On Angels' Wings

A Journey Through Alzheimer's with My Mother

Deborah Lynn

Balboa Press books may be ordered through booksellers or by contacting:

Balboa Press
A Division of Hay House
1663 Liberty Drive
Bloomington, IN 47403
www.balboapress.com
1 (877) 407-4847

Print information available on the last page.

ISBN: 978-1-5043-7513-9 (sc)
ISBN: 978-1-5043-7550-4 (e)

Library of Congress Control Number: 2017902752

Balboa Press rev. date: 05/08/2017

To my mother, my muse

And to every invisible caregiver inside their invisible suffering,
the suffering of their quiet love

Table of Contents

List of Illustrations

Barbara Durling Miller January 16, 1923 - January 12, 2015

Preface

Here

My mother wrote this book with me.
She held my hand, I stroked her hair
Read her each word with somber care —
From her bed, and wheelchair bound,
She mused me through every word I found.

Encased in myriad details here
Our journey does unfold

My mother, angel, always,
Now and for eternity,
We celebrate our story.

Every piece of art has a story–not the story that it tells, but the story that it *is:* how it came to be in the mind and heart of the artist. Every work of art displays a part of the soul of its creator.

To me, poetry is painting with words, and painting–graphic artistry–is poetry without words. I love the lilting flow, the sound and deeper meaning of words as much as the artist is enamored with each stroke of the brush or curve, line and color of their piece. All these flow directly from the heart of their creator, bringing a piece of someone's soul to light for you to see and hear and experience in your own being. Sharing these parts of our souls and lives with each other enriches our journey here on this earth.

Because of this, what I intended to be a collection of poetry became this story, this journey, to share with you. The very first time I sat down with my writing group to put these poems together, I knew I had to tell their story. I knew that what I had to share with you was more than the out-pouring of my heart and soul through the imagery of my poetry; it was the the prose of our everyday lives. Here you will find our journey, my mother's and mine, traced through the dark despairing days of this deadly disease as it robbed us slowly and inexorably of everything we had known in our relationship, journeying together into a place of new relationship and healing.

And so, instead of a collection of poetry which–while beautiful to read, is sometimes disconnected from its context–I have woven you a full piece; a background of prose illustrated with poetry and art.

This is our story, our journey, Mom's and mine. I invite you to join us.

At the beginning of each chapter I have featured work from artist Peggy McClure's collections entitled "Shadows" and "Forces of Nature." Each piece reached out to me in my struggles and spoke, without words, of our journey. Alzheimer's is a journey of Shadows attended by immutable Forces of Nature.

The heart-and-wings logo detail found throughout the book was custom designed for me. It and the nature photographs at the beginning and end are by artist Ellen Keiter.

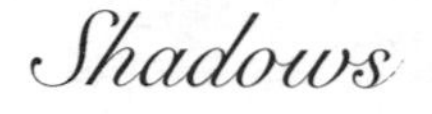

The shadows of our lives
in colors undescribed
fall softly, quietly in time.
This turn, then that, now
a mountain to climb of
fear or hope or heaven.
They stretch and lengthen over years,
take on shapes that only dimly appear
to be what they really mean.

Who can into a lifetime peer,
find its true qualities seen
in the dimly lit shadows
of its suffering?

Only the reflection of a thing
is ever there
as if it would our sight impair
to fully grasp reality.

In the shadows of a life lived,
learned,
crisp and dark
or dimly set
are Wisdom's truths, life's deep best in the shadows,
at rest.

Acknowledgments

My Dream Factory Community:

When first presenting a pre-publication peek to my wonderful women at one of our gatherings, I titled my talk "It Takes a Community to Write a Book!" I am deeply grateful to this unique and wonderful community of women who have been my mentors, muses, coaches, guides and supporters throughout the long journey of this book. During my struggles walking through this disease with Mom, as I discovered and connected with my poetic heart, and while I wrote and assembled this book, they have been my constant supporters, admirers and valued colleagues.

Connie Dunn (Publish with Connie) and my writing group:

As soon as I sat down in my group to put together my poetry, this book expanded way beyond my original conception of it. Within this safe, supportive group, aptly facilitated by Connie, ideas and dreams grew, and received the input and support needed to become so much bigger and better than anything first imagined! Many thanks!

My husband, Arthur:

Bless him! He cooked and cleaned, loved and supported and never complained, no matter how much I was absent from him to be with my writing, my mother and my work. If he had not been there to take care of thousands of daily details with love and support, this book would have taken much longer to create.

Rick Duthie:

My very-first-ever editor! Many thanks for being so gentle and for making my sometimes extemporaneous and impulsive flow of thoughts and feelings into a smooth-flowing, gentle river of story.

Ellen Keiter:

What do I say here? For countless hours spent in her warm and welcoming home, with my new friend, Deke, a huge black Lab mix, guarding the door to the office where Ellen and I worked over this manuscript page by page, period by period, thought by thought. For her partner Billy's patience as I usurped Ellen for hours on end, for his occasional comments and insights, and constant support. For all the gluten-free food, bottles of wine, and wise advise. For her careful, detailed eye over the presentation of every page, the meaning of every line, the beauty of every word in print. I found a consummate and demanding artist in Ellen, and could not have entrusted the design and final editing of this beloved work to a finer guide.

Introduction

There is something amazing and all-consuming about walking through the death of your mother. She gave you life, sheltered, protected and grew you inside her. She labored over your birth and dedicated her being, breath and strength, creativity, hope, prosperity and life—both present and future—to your growth, health, nurture, teaching, care and guidance. Then she opened her hand and let you go, sending and surrounding you every minute and moment with her spirit, love and care. When she expires—leaves this earth—her leaving can be a process of spiritual growth and preparation taking time and care, as was your own birth and growth into adulthood. As she prepares to leaves this life, you may feel a deep desire, almost a compelling commission, to give her the same care, love, commitment, sacrifice and service that she gave to present you, whole, to the world.

You are given the chance to give back to eternity the goddess who gave you life.
The circle of love is unending.

Part One
The Journey

Beginnings . . .

What did I know
In the beginning so—
A child of fantasy and glow—
How could I perceive the layers of life
Or see into a grown-up strife?

Yet all around in swirling cares
I felt her worries in the air
And breathed unhappiness in her stare.
A longing, faraway look she had. . . .

Covered over with all her skill,
A pleasant homemaker, she set her will
To be the picture-perfect
Wife and mother of her time. . . .

No one knew her inner clime,
Only my sister and I.
How much those sorrows set her edge,
Paved her journey to this page,
A woman bereft in her heart.

We'll never know just where the start
Of any ending is,
We only look, surmise,
And wonderingly comprise
A beginning somewhere. . . .

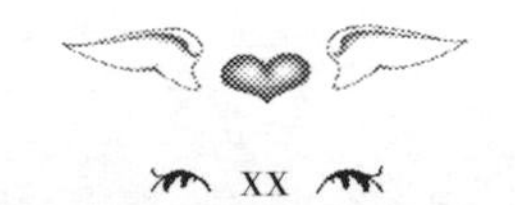

On Angels' Wings

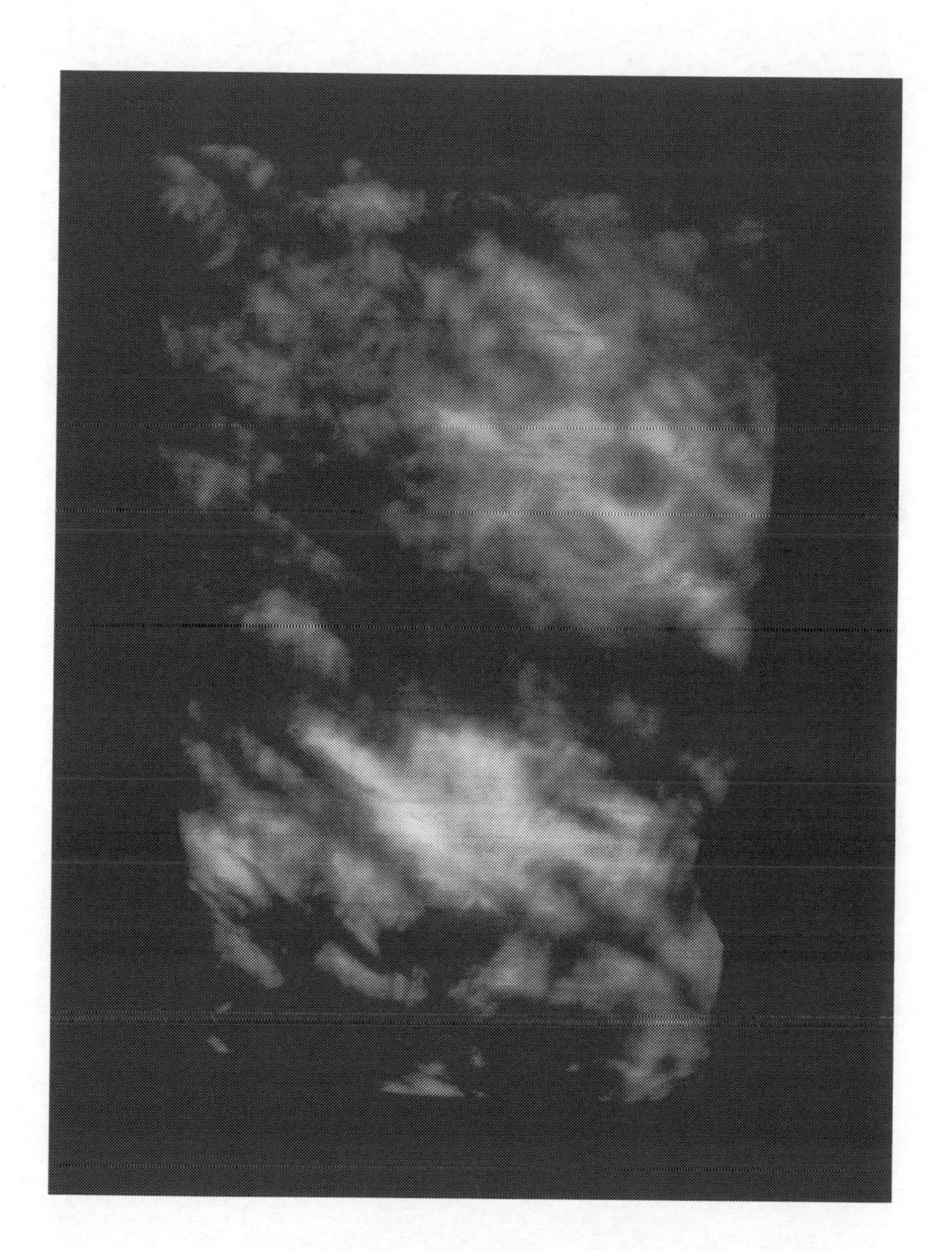

Shadows I

Chapter One

The Beginning

How to start? Where to start?
One must always start at the beginning. . . .

Yet, like Alzheimer's itself, beginnings can be hard to perceive. Sometimes, they are many disparate little things that either all of a sudden, or slowly over time, come together like a woven pattern in a piece, begin to take on color and shape and meaning—and then you perceive a beginning.

Only when you stand back from a thing in space or time does it take its shape, hold its color, become meaning-filled. When we are solidly face-to-face with daily interactions, the patterns of our lives are sometimes too close to be discerned.

Was there a beginning to Mom's Alzheimer's? There was. Buried somewhere in the tenuous strands and filaments of her brain, delicate protein fibers began to grow. They grew and grew and stretched and grew until they started to choke the spaces between her neurons, interrupting the paths of energy and thought and flow, and causing memories to disappear; but these events were far too deep and too subtle for us to perceive. For us, on the outside looking in, perception began when we slowly noticed that things with Mom were not as they used to be. There were odd behaviors and actions that we were swift to chalk up to her being older, or more bitter, or what ever other reason we could imagine or suppose.

There will always be clouds—
No matter how bright the sun of life begun,
It's fun and joy perceived, believed . . .
There are always clouds that come. . . .

Blindness . . . or how we wanted everything to be normal, or wanted it to be Mom's fault and character defects, and how it was really disease. . . .

Being "the child," I did not feel comfortable speaking openly about what I saw, but my husband voiced his concern right away. Coming out of the bathroom during one of our visits he commented to me that Mom had sticky notes all over the house–including the bathroom. She started calling me to come down to help her organize her attic storage spaces–this from a woman who had not only raised her family and run her house, but also worked as executive secretary to the head of the local hospital.

Standing back and looking at the events of these years, I am no longer flattered by her attention and apparent elevation of me from the status of child to cohort. (In our family, one was forever thought of as "the child.") Now I see more clearly the pattern of disease that was slowly forming before our ever-willing-to-be-blind eyes. My sister claimed the cause was Mom's grief and anger over losing her second husband so suddenly. We have since learned that such traumas can accelerate or even cause the onset of this disease, as if hiding in the wings, waiting for its cue.

Whatever the trigger, her journey–and ours–had begun.

Disconnected

From the world around
My inner self abounds,
Invites my inner eye to see
Vast glimpses of reality
And truths too hard to tell . . .

Heartfelt, they swell
Beneath the quiet calm
I, to my outward world propel.
Who knows the thoughts and heart that dwell
Within the soul's deep well?

My sister became indignant at Mom's sometimes "loose-cannon" remarks. There came a time when the two of them battled over children, grandchildren, issues . . . anything. I remember my mother commenting sadly and a bit tartly about her goings-on with my sister. I remember thinking it very unusual for my sister to be at odds with my mother over everything, as the two of them had always been close as "peas in a pod"–while I, standing on the outside, had usually disagreed over "the way things should be done."

I secretly gloated; it was about time they had some bumps and I had smooth sailing. Who knew that personality changes and lack of verbal self-control were signs of this insidious disease? We thought it was all "just Mom."

Butterflies—Butterflies

Seen upon the wing,
My, aren't they such pretty things!
Dancing, dancing on the air
Unseen fairy breath
Just beyond perception's depth
Bringing hope near death,
Just by being there.

Butterflies—butterflies
Dancing on the air
Oh, keep us near your vision clear
Of beauty, love and life—
Especially when our souls descend
To murky darkness 'round the bend
Lost our sight in pain again.

Lift our vision on your wings
Bring our minds to higher things
Let our heart-souls follow there
Up in clearer, shining air.

Light and lilting, burden-free
Lifted on the breeze to see
Over the mountain and past the stream
Into the future of our dreams.
Where do you take us? Take us there!
Calm and soothed as hope on air
Lifted gently from our care
Beautiful spirits of life!

Shadows II

Chapter Two

Life is a Mystery

Life is a mystery—not just your mystery, the one about figuring yourself out; it is the mystery of tracing not only your footsteps, but also the footsteps of your mother, your grandmother and those before her. These are not just roots. Sometimes in this journey, I have the feeling we are all on our paths at the same time. If I stop and look to my left or right through the misty, cool, dimly lit woods of life, I will see my mother's path. Sometimes I see her in different places in her life on that path, sometimes only her footsteps and I know she has been this way. Beyond her I see my beloved grandmother Daisy, more dimly and farther away in the misty woods. We are all paralleling one another—not that our paths are exactly the same. They weave in and out, closer and farther away—and I know that my mother and grandmother have each dealt with the same challenges of life, the same emotional, spiritual and life tasks that compose my own journey. And they have also dealt with Alzheimer's.

As I wonder about my own future, and whether or not it holds Alzheimer's for me as well, it is comforting to see their footsteps, to look through to their time, to see them paused upon their paths over a particularly difficult part, and say: I wonder if my mother felt this way? How did my grandmother handle this? What did she feel, think? What determined her steps?

There is strength in the shared passions of our lives across generations. There is the whispering echo of their voices—their encouragement, their courage. They have gone before, and I take strength in that.

Ode to Women

The spirit of woman,
Proud and unpossessed
Seen from an eagle's eye
Not from the nest.

Soaring, unfettered, unlimited in the sky,
Spirits of courage and wisdom and try,
Those who have nothing that meets the eye,
No beauty or strength we can see or apply—
These are the women who know how to fly.

Once released from their limits
Like fledglings on air
Filled with spirit
They strive and they dare.

These are the women to whom we owe honor,
The honor of courage and trying and care,
The ones we have heard of, their stories our song.
We look to the heights, to where they have flown
And measure our steps with the might they have grown.

Oh, women of youth, age and birth—
Tenders and lovers, the mothers of earth
Do not faint, do not falter,
Stand fast in the gate
Midwifing each thought to eternity's place
To view with a limitless eye and heart
The rhythms of life as they end and start.

Bring your wisdom, your courage,
Your strength and your love—
Their hearts are such that we stand in their glow
And slowly perceiving the paths that they've sown—
An ode, a tribute, a triumph, a song
To the women of now and of then, long gone
Who labored, created, and built us along
On legacies left of spirit and song.

Break loose, break fast, break free, be gone.
Oh, be not fettered beyond the dawn!
Their strength and spirit is freely passed on.
Take up the "Yes!" and join their throng!

My Grandmother Daisy . . .

I have a picture of my grandmother, grandfather, and their four daughters on my bureau. I have four daughters. My grandmother and I each bore four daughters.

My mother's mother was Daisy Durling. She was the first adult in my life who listened to me and accepted me as an adult. She did not treat me like a child when I outgrew childhood. A veteran of the days of Vaudeville, she met my grandfather on the stage and came to America with him, from their native England. He used to sing "A Bicycle Built for Two" to her when I was growing up. To me, it was their love song. My grandfather died when I was sixteen, and my grandmother died at ninety-four of Alzheimer's years later when I was thirty. I remember visiting her in the nursing home, hearing the stories of how my aunt could no longer care for her, and the family commenting over what was happening and who was at fault. My grandmother no longer knew us when we came to visit, but I remember having parties with her when her daughters and granddaughters were all around her and she beamed with joy in the presence of the love of all the beautiful women surrounding her.

I had a dream about my grandmother after she died. I was worried because she seemed so agitated. I saw her pressing through a dark curtain to the other side, and knew that, though it was a tough crossing, she made it.

Goodbye for now,
The cares of life left below.
Thanks for all the hugs you bestowed.
It's up on them I'm sure you rose.
I'll see you there someday, I know.
You'll be with Mom,
Watching there for me,
Keeping an eye on eternity!

I loved my Grandma Daisy. I wore her mustard seed necklace in my wedding, I have daisies planted all around my house, and one of my daughters was married on a warm July afternoon, with the daisy as her wedding flower.

My grandmother's oldest daughter, my Aunt Shirley, died from Alzheimer's a while back. I remember my mother remarking that she was now the oldest living member of her family. As of this writing her two younger twin sisters are in early and mid-stage Alzheimer's disease. This is a dreaded bond shared by the women in my family. We don't even ask where it comes from—we simply take up the chore of caring for the one who cared for us. The Mystery is, where do our paths go from here? Somewhere out there in the misty woods of the future, where the footsteps of our elders have already left their impression, will be my path . . . and yours. Look well to the right and left as you travel; even if you do not know where you are going, know where you are.

May day
Overcome the fears of night,
Ground-store of darkness that blinds our sight.
May hope
And vision stir our hearts
With the wisdom they impart.
Lift the blinds
On torn strands of time,
Weave the light
Of paths divine,
Guide us gently as we go,
Causing faith, hope and love
To grow.

Shadows III

Chapter Three

Confusion: Hers

And so, I'll bring a poem to thee
written on a glassy sea
of days and times that used to be,
of songs we sang, both you and me. . . .

Mom continued, delightfully confused in gentle ways, unnoticed, hidden, for years. Steeped from her youth in the art of creating the appearance of properness, niceness, showing only her best face to the world, she continued her lonely journey. Recently widowed, she was conveniently alone. Always having been an extremely competent and capable mother, wife, hostess and businesswoman, she had the perfect facade behind which to retreat. No one would ever suspect. No one did. In 2001, when she was seventy-eight, she married a lovely man, Tom, who simply thought of her as, yes, slightly confused, while all the time she was slowly losing her grasp on things in ways only she was aware of.

When I first saw her living will, read its words about becoming unable to care for herself or live with dignity, and noted its date, April 1997, I knew she knew. Mom was no fool. She was seventy-four years old and she knew something was wrong. It was later that very same year that she first asked for my help organizing around her house.

Watching the sheer intelligence and wit with which she coped with Alzheimer's was one of the most amazing experiences I had with Mom once her disease was diagnosed in 2006. It gave me a much deeper respect for her. There are still notes in her handwriting all over the house. She wrote them to tell us what she knew she would not be able to remember later. "Your father's baby knife. It's the only piece I have left of his set." "Diane and Debbie's baby spoons, give to Rebecca's first baby and Victoria's" (her granddaughters).

Who knew what she lived with in all those years of knowing and not sharing?

She stopped being a docent at Heritage Plantation. Then she stopped singing with the Saints and Singers, her beloved choral group, claiming she did not like the music, or did not want to sing second soprano or alto after years of singing soprano. She faded away from the garden club, stopped writing her letters to the editor, and we went blithely on—unconscious—conveniently distracted with our families and our lives, leaving her to show her brave facade to the world.

I am so glad she had those few lovely years with her new husband, Tom, in the early 2000's. At the time, I was relieved she had found him, as I was concerned about her confusion. Yet I still never had a conscious thought about something being seriously wrong. Neither did my sister nor Tom. We were serenely blind. And somewhere behind that lovely facade, Mom was all alone with her knowledge.

Ode to Alzheimer's Patients

Going away, by minutes and hours and days,
exiting life without that grace
and presence of mind with which to save face,
helping hands reach out to break your fall
guide you carefully, stumbling all
over huge unknowns,
blocks of soul, like stones
unseen
tripping and catching us in between.

Each staring turn we try to make—
no one is an expert here,
each path is different, jumbled and unclear
with patient's disease and family's fright
staring into the blacker-than-night
unknown,
the mystery of Alzheimer's grown

Softly, silently, treacherously—
a robber stealing what we cannot see:
seconds and minutes and hours and days
quietly slipping away. Suddenly done,
bereft and forlorn, we stand looking back
at our empty hands—
unable to grasp what is truly
gone.

A loved one departs in front of our eyes,
minute by minute counts their demise.
We comfort, delay, and hedge them about

with all the trappings medicine can spout,
and still stand amazed in an empty space
when we finally glimpse the loss of that place
where a mind with its life
used to be.

Somehow, we tell ourselves,
I thought there was more of them left
than this.

When we finally gaze, clear-eyed through the mist,
we see the great courage and challenge they faced
peering out at us from lost inner space,
making us and themselves
feel as normal as they can,
all the while holding deep their own loss
in its span.

A brave, lonely walk, each hour and minute,
each Alzheimer's patient has faced,
and traced for us here
in the sands of time
their journey long gone from the depths of
their mind.

By seconds, and minutes and hours and days
each counterpoint slipping silent away—
sometimes they knew it,
reached out to hold on—
sometimes like a ghost,
in the dawn, it was gone. . . .

Bid them tell their stories well,
laugh at their moments, fill
your cup with their joy.
You will walk in its light
as the path grows most dim,
use its glow to guide them as long as you can—
blessed people of minutes and hours and days
slipping slowly,
completely,
forever,
away.

Pulling Aside the Curtain

Chapter Four

The Pain of Truth

And now,
a gentle lullaby
to soothe your savoried soul,
I'll bring around a candle cloud
to light your way back home.

In 2005, Mom developed diverticulitis. By Easter 2006, after her second attack requiring hospitalization, I drove down from Boston to Cape Cod to make sure she was okay before she and Tom took off to Florida for an Easter visit with Tom's son and his family.

She wasn't okay.

Mom's colon had burst, and it was an anxious early morning run to the emergency room the morning after I got there. Mom was weakly signing her health proxy papers. Tom had left to go back home and collect some things, and my older sister was on her way down to meet us. All alone I stood by Mom as the doctor came in and said she needed a colostomy–immediately. Time stood still, and then turned upside down, as the baby of the family signed her mother away.

I agonizingly concluded that the anesthesia from the operations that ensued accelerated her disease. Later we learned from a compassionate doctor that what the anesthesia really does is unmask the disease. This was small comfort. Whatever the truth, the result was no longer deniable. Mom had become, at eighty-three, and almost overnight to our blinded eyes, a vague, unknowing being, unable to determine where she was and what had happened. Her memory was clearly gone. I went online, madly researching the disease and its causes, contacted the Alzheimer's Association, and horrifyingly pegged her at mid-stage of the disease.

I remember thinking, much later, that my wild run down to see her then probably saved her life; but it also consigned her to living through the full course of Alzheimer's that we were blessed with upon her recovery. The pain and soft sadness of seeing her mind and abilities slip inexorably away in the ensuing years—despite everything and anything that medical expertise and personal love and connection could do—was heart-rending.

Pain

Now I know why Jackie O
Wore those big dark glasses . . .
Deep inside
Where you can hide
Behind the shades of day
Chasing pain and sorrow away . . .
Drop the blinds
Go inside
Work your way to safety—
Keep them out
Peering doubt
Hold your song—sing it loud
Don the shades 'gainst sightless rays
Of those who would your passions rob
Feel your own heart throb.

Sit with it softly,
Till, balance restored,
You can walk again
Amongst the paths of men.
Close the shutters
Drop the blinds
Sit with your pain
Till it subsides . . .
Peaceful,
Perceive the rising tide
Welcome the shore,
The ocean's roar—
Let pain go with its ebb and flow
Until you know
It's safe, to open the door.

After Mom came home from the hospital, there began a series of heartbreaking phone calls—I came to call them *plateau calls.* From far away my mother's voice would reassure me that she would remember all of her bankers that she had somehow forgotten after Tom had reintroduced her to them. She then proceeded to tell me she could remember how to sign her checks but did not know what they were for. I insisted on being present at the next medical meeting to suggest to her doctor–with Tom and my sister present and without Mom there–that Tom be given power of attorney. The doctor immediately agreed. Tom and my sister appeared appalled that I would mention such a thing, and were, I am sure, caught by surprise when the doctor supported the idea. I felt so alone, as if I was the only one who was hearing–really hearing–the disease speak.

Then followed phone calls from Mom about working the oven, or turning down the air conditioning while Tom was out working at his part-time job. I told her to wait for Tom to get home, that he would help her. Later, came a poignant call. She wanted to make sure that Tom was remembered in her will because he was taking such good care of her. I reassured her that all was well, that she had put everything in place. One day, she just wanted to talk about what was going on, why she was trying so hard to find memories that were no longer there. I finally told her she had Alzheimer's disease, like her mother. She was not upset. She was, momentarily, relieved. She said, "Oh, is that what this is?" Can you imagine the mystery of waking up to find parts of yourself gone each day? She searched for them like lost jewels upon the shore.

I called these plateau calls because most often she was chasing the tail end of being able to remember that she once knew something; she was calling me to fill in the blank spaces before her memory dropped off to the next plateau where she would not remember that she used to know it –whatever it was.

We watched helplessly as the disease progressed and she recessed, like a receding tide, from life, as we were able to walk and talk it with her each day, to a place where it was much harder to join or walk with her.

Slowly, Tom became everything and everyone in her life . . . her primary caregiver.

Places

Watching places disappear,
Your plants are gone,
They are not here.

The clutter of your life is cleared
As softly, gently you release
And trust another for your care,
Parts of your cupboard have gone bare.

He gently removes,
Simplifies
What is there.

Yet every time I visit
Your home has one less you.

The magazines no longer crowd
Invitingly on table tops
The furniture's moved,
The books are gathered,
Everything is "tidied up."

And slowly I perceive how much
You filled your space, expressed yourself
In myriad minuscule ways.

Impacting on my universe, your personality replays
In thousands of tiny unknowns,
Filtering through my days.

No wonder we were comfortable in each other's lives,
Intertwined like ivy, roots dug deep—the same.

I miss your place
Your personality's space. . . .

Expressed around you now
We feebly build our tribute,
Hedging you about
With comforting objects to recreate
The memories we've lost
And keep you painted with
The colors
We hold and cherish most.

As I write these words, I am sitting in her "her spot" on her couch after one of my nursing home visits to her, with her husband Tom sitting across the room in his chair watching a football game. There is something wonderful and very fitting about being here in her space as I pen her journey for you.

I wrote the next poem on the Mother's Day before Mom went into the nursing home in 2010– my final gift of homage that she was aware enough to hear with both her heart and mind. This was a crucial communication for both of us. Not only did I pour out parts of my heart to her that I had not been able to express before, but I also signaled to her that I had reconnected with my writing after decades of silence. A love of writing as self-expression is one of the quintessential qualities we continued to share on our journey together through Alzheimer's.

Owed to My Mother

Thank you!
You birthed me.
It was a lot for you to do—
It meant a lot to me, too!

Thank you, for binding up my boo-boos,
Healing up my hurts.
All those hugs and kisses,
and wiping off the dirt!

In splashy bubble baths,
playing with my toys,
lazy afternoons spent out of doors.

You held my hand when I was scared
you sat through school plays and you dared
that wet sponge ace
at my circus party, to aim straight
at Dad, who got dunked in place!
Oh, we laughed till we split over his surprise
That some little kid could put him over the side!

You let me climb tall trees
play in the fields
dress up my dolls
make my room into—anything at all . . .

I remember, I remember—
I was born in September,
beautiful last month of summer,
with bell-clear warm and balmy weather

You Virgo-ed me, mothered me, sang to me
blessed me.
Thank you.

You made me coats and jackets
knit me my favorite hat—it
became too small
as I became so big and tall.

Stand up straight, you said!
Keep your shoulders back, chin up,
getting me ready to be grown up.
Thanks for taking such good care of me

For watching out and being ware for me,
for trepidaciously letting me go
when I took off and left fast and sudden so—

Your heart must have pounded
not knowing which fears were ungrounded,
Whether I would fly or fall,
or ever even get there at all.

Thanks for all the prayers you sent;
they left a trail for my ascent
so when I look back now at bumps and falls
none of them seem to have taken their toll.

Your love smoothed out the way when I didn't know it at all.

Thanks for taking such good care of me!
I remember, I remember now, you see.
I remember, you and me.

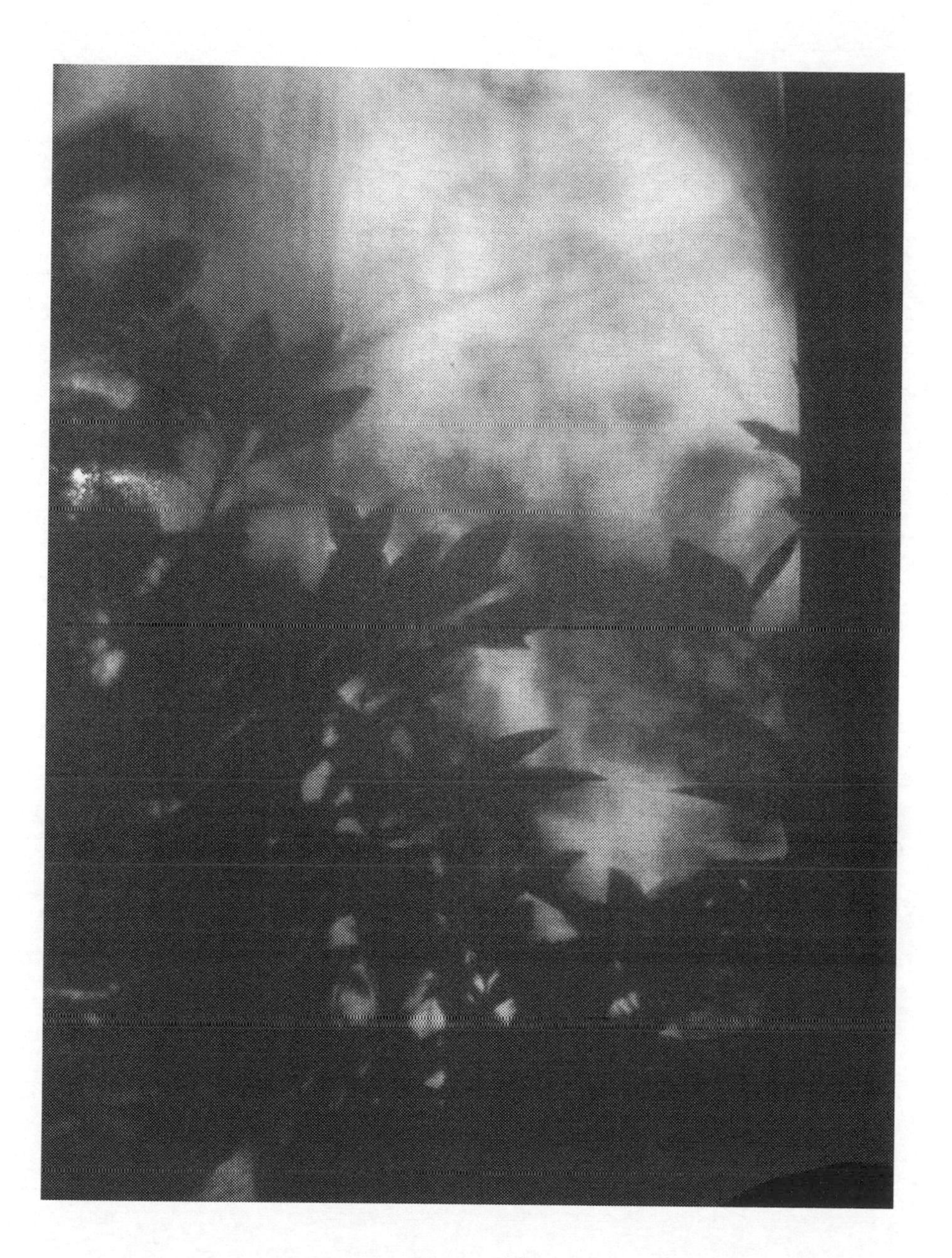

Shadow IV

Chapter Five

Tom's Story

And yet, I love you very much—
so much it hurts, you see,
I'll love you always, every day
from now to eternity. . . .

And who lived with her every day? Who faced the endless questions, repeated at two minute intervals, "Tom, where did you put the jam?" when she opened the refrigerator door forgetting she had just been there?

Who came home from the short-lived relief of a three-hour workday after leaving her set with lunch and music only to find she'd taken all the clothes out of her closet again; and who then patiently put them back for her?

Who struggled to pick out her food and her clothes, dress her and groom her when she lost interest and had forgotten how to do these simple daily tasks?

Who found her in bed in the middle of the day because she thought it was the night?

Who sadly closed up the jewelry case when she no longer remembered to wear her beloved rings and earrings? Who learned how to brush, wash and trim her hair when she could no longer tolerate the trip to her hairdresser?

Who learned to give her simple sets of instructions, be constantly on call for the need of the moment; exhausted himself to make her feel and be safe, secure and loved; answered endless phone calls when she could no longer remember she had just called him?

Who got up with her during night wanderings, cleaned up, took care of her needs following the colostomy until the procedure was reversed?

Who learned that he had to tell her what she liked to eat when she was out, reminded her to use her silverware, watered her plants, washed her laundry and cooked her meals?

Who doled out her medications, took her to doctors' appointments, wrote notes, and worried constantly over every daily detail?

Who cared for the yard and house, paid the bills and watched over the finances?

Who watched with saddened horror as his care-taking became no longer enough? Who took her to work with him to keep her safe and calm those last few months? Finally, one Sunday morning she slipped through the fingers of his care and flitted out the door before he could distract her: out the door and down the driveway, he following–the pair of them in their bathrobes–in early Sunday morning madness, until, as she fended him off as if a stranger, he hauntingly pleading over her shoulder to an astonished neighbor, "Call 911"?

And who wept when he got back to his car in the parking lot after every visit to the nursing home, feeling as though he had somehow not done enough?

And if we part, as ere we must—
but never from the heart—
a kiss,
a hug,
and restful be
my own true love,
forever, thee.

My sister and I are eternally grateful to Tom for keeping our mother peaceful, safe, secure and at home for as long as he possibly could.

And the true sadness of this is, you see, that he felt he had failed her in some awful way when she finally had to go to the nursing home. He truly thought she was not as far along in her journey through Alzheimer's as she was, and felt that he had made a poor showing by not being able to keep her home longer.

In the Nursing Home

Sadness ends, beginning bends
back upon itself.
Memory delves in mystic swirls—
the mind is a thing that twirls
in unexpected ways unnamed, unclaimed,
unmapped—a chartless sea of second guesses,
lost entrances,
a place to be we cannot see
when mind grows dim.

Sadness, loss
I cannot follow there,
that place you go to
in there somewhere,
where your mind has bent
and sent you off.
I cannot be there with you now,
I wish I could, somehow.

Blessings, peace, wherever you are,
we'll meet again at journey's end—
sadness now, gladness then!
I love you, Mom. Amen.

Once Mom was in the nursing home, one long struggle ended; then another began. There is no rest for the caregiver in this disease. Tom began the battle for Medicaid coverage. Even with a very good elder-care lawyer, the process was exhausting. It took nine months to get coverage. Meanwhile, my sister, Tom and I, as her designated health care proxies, went through many unforeseen twists and turns, ups and downs in the roller coaster ride of nursing home navigation. All of these set us constantly on edge in our drawn-out commission to bring the best possible care to Mom.

Once coverage was securely in place and several changes of venue accomplished for Mom, Tom had literally been through a year of physical breakdown, injuries and illnesses that reflected the mental, physical and emotional depletion he had been through. He eventually regained his strength. Many times with older couples, the caretaker actually dies first, and indeed, Tom himself felt, at one point soon after Mom had been placed in the nursing home, that she would outlive him. My husband and I had seen this happen several times within our own circle of older friends. My sister and I and our families were committed to loving and supporting both Mom and Tom throughout this journey.

One of my greatest regrets is that I feel I did not try hard enough to encourage Tom to make use of the resources available to him through the Alzheimer's Association and the various programs and community groups that could have provided him with help during Mom's at-home stages of the illness. The Alzheimer's Association provides education about the disease, empowering the caregiver to prepare and be knowledgeable in their daily challenges. There are social outings to museums and movies available through Art for Alzheimer's and other community-based programs, home health care facilities that provide support and help for the at-home caregiver and even respite care programs where a trusted person stays with the loved one while the caregiver takes some quiet time, runs errands, or does whatever is needed. My sister and I, while close enough to visit and provide planned times of care, were just far enough away from Mom and Tom to make it an unfeasible undertaking to ride down to relieve him for a few moments of precious time on a regular basis. I would have been happier knowing he had that little bit of extra support.

Love

Climbing to heaven
on angel stairs
carrying you,
safe within
the loving womb
of time and care,
the curling wings
of a thousand prayers. . . .

Shadows V

Chapter Six

Denial
or The Family Feud Over Care

Families either come together or break apart over challenges and dangers. It's not that ours fell apart, but that I did not always come together with it. Somehow, my ways were not their ways. . . .

Nothing showed this more clearly than watching our responses in 2006 to the unmasking of Mom's disease. The three of us, Tom, my sister and I, had completely different opinions on what was needed. I was heroically ready to face the decisions and amass the resources needed to move forward collaboratively in the upcoming challenges of meeting Mom's and Tom's needs as they moved through Alzheimer's disease together. I was met with huge resistance–not the confrontational or direct disagreement kind, but the delicate backing off, clearing one's throat and gentle putting aside from plans and discussions and care. I was politely left out.

The issue here was perceiving, understanding, and living in the reality of where Mom was in her disease.

I felt we needed to acknowledge the disease and get help from outside resources to enrich Mom's life and experience as she went through this middle stage, and to get help for Tom. My sister and Tom felt that Mom was in the early stages, since the disease had just been diagnosed, and that I was certainly overdoing it. Theirs was a need to keep everything just as it was until it became undeniably apparent that a change was needed. Tom was sure he could handle everything and seemed unwilling to use outside help. This became the chosen course and, to my perception, it resulted in unpreparedness when those inevitable changes came: decisions based on an innacurate assessment of the level of her disease, and the lack of some wonderful life-enriching opportunities that might have been there for Mom. But then, the real question is, what would she have chosen for herself had she been able to? Very likely she would have wished to stay behind the curtains and keep the illusion going. Very likely the decisions to stay away from anything to do with an open acknowledgment of Alzheimer's and use of community resources would have been her own choice, too. Mom and I did not always agree on things or see them from the same point of view. . . .

There followed a period of disconnection, where Tom and my sister took over most of Mom's care and oversight, without much communication to me. I could have been more present for this time, but did not want to be a continuing voice of dissent; I simply chose to accept not being part of Mom's daily care and health decisions. I was working full-time and my sister had more time available to help out. Her pharmacist husband provided input on medications and all seemed to be going well. Perhaps because I was not as continuously involved as they were, I noticed the progression of Mom's Alzheimer's keenly and was concerned, yet did not feel it was my place to speak. My sister and I did not communicate well during this time and I frequently booked holidays for our family with Mom and Tom separately, allowing space in between. I realized Mom was easily overwhelmed by these family gatherings, which were now too much for her to handle.

This was all most difficult and delicate to go through, while keeping the focus on what really mattered: Mom and Tom.

Hang on Mom! We're trying!
Working it out, crying,
but letting go a little bit slow . . .

I have actually heard that our struggles to cope with each other through this time were relatively mild. Some families are at war over a loved one's care. It's a matter of our individual approaches to the grief, fear and pain we face, and how those play out differently–jarring against one another in the working out of end-of-life care for one who can no longer express his or her own wishes.

Albatross

Letting go with love . . .
a difficult thing to do.
If there were just some algorithm,
an equation or two,
that worked in every case and true,
just plug anything into x, y and z
and find the easier path to eternity.

Instead we hang and grope about
dark alleyways of fear and doubt
counting out our lot and shout
with pain and agonizing tear,
figuring out how to get from here to there . . .

Completely fractured at endpoint,
even Christians quake
at just how that final step to take.

Decisions to prolong or release
become a case for court and press,
because we do not dare to guess
at what awaits end's assured fate
when loved ones leave us at life's gate
and pass through where we cannot see.

Ah, would it not a different reality be
if only a verifiable glimpse might prove
death does not existence end,
just some part of it, knowing, bends
to sight and sense unseen,
and travels on unbroken in between?

Let's not hold back at the starting gate
because to us it's the end of the race!
A kiss, a hug, love's light embrace
letting go with God's good grace,
knowing it is we who stand
back where our loved ones
mourn for us our loss,
held back from this, the way across.

We on the shores, an albatross
of fear and blindness to the cost
slung trophy-like round our necks,
pushed back from what comes next:
the beautiful life of heaven's rest,
its freedoms seen as too much to bear
to wrest us from our burdens here. . . .

The Resolution . . .

Ironically enough, I got my mother back when she went into nursing home care. Because I was one of her health care proxies, and she was no longer cloistered at home, I became a voice in her assessment and care from that point on.

It was in these final chapters of her life that I re-entered the stage and played my lines. Loving and caring and spirit-aware, I searched and pursued every active field to engage and enliven her soul and spirit, even as her mind slipped farther away.

Spirit Women

Spirit Women—hawks in flight
overhead in ever sight
symbols of eternity
women flying
ever free
Soar—soar
and scream at me
"Don't you see? Don't you see?
Earth's hastening to eternity.
Listen—listen—to me!"

Spirit works in a straight line
Listen—it is divine—
a gift—to hear
what those who are dear
say when they've "lost their minds."
They leave us clues behind,
point to all that's fine . . .
and truly in their minds.

I felt as if I was lilting a dance around her in the air, weaving a web of love and care. It was nice to see my silver glistening strands reflecting rainbow light entwined within her care. She smiled when I was there. Her eyes lit, she blew me kisses, and we met. I read her poetry, sang her songs, brought her soft flowers to feel and smell, drew pictures, rubbed her hands with sweet creams, had tea parties–just the two of us. I was there so that any of her moments I could fill might be filled with joy, awareness, connecting. She had so much sadness and disappointment in her life; the disease actually became a friend that erased her capacity for bitterness, and thereby opened her to joy. She became my muse, listening to my words and nodding her head; she knew that I was writing our story. She guided me to her files when I told her about this book. Her memory might be gone the next second after we met, but in those moments of meeting, time was light, peaceful, clear and connected.

Spirit

Spirit Sight
filled with might,
glowing auras of your light
sent on angels' wings, prayers, love
they travel through, come from above
to fill and grant you peace and hugs.

You and me, in a place we can be
unburdened by life's fragility—
I'll meet you there, Mom, while you're here
in space and spirit, cool and clear.
We'll touch and kiss and hold each dear
wrapped within the spirit's sphere. . . .

I love you, Mom!
Come be with me!
I invite you into eternity—
serene and soaring like birds of the sea,
those beautiful gulls you've longed to be.
We're here! We're there!
Flying clear—holding hands in ecstasy!
Isn't it delightful to be free?

Take my love back with you
when you slip back into self,
glow with sunlight, sleep with rest,
knowing love-light holds you best!

Descending

Chapter Seven

The Nursing Home Nightmare

I apologize to every nursing home facility and their staff.
I know they may find this title offensive, but this was our nightmare. . . .

Working together at last in this final stage, my sister and I were a formidable force in standing for the level of care and treatment we felt was healthful for Mom. This is a must in nursing home life. But honestly, there occurred a horrible succession of facilities—first a nursing home, then an assisted-living facility, and finally an inappropriate rehab center—before we settled Mom back into in a particular unit of her first facility that provided for her needs and care in a manner acceptable to us. This was due mostly to an early lack of preparation for and awareness of her true stage in the disease, and what she really needed. Mom (and we, too) could easily have been spared much of the agony of the first year of her nursing home life if plans had been made with an open-eyed awareness of her condition earlier on in the decision-making process.

Our nursing home story is a clear illustration of the blind-sightedness of denial at work in the approach to Alzheimer's disease and care. I remember being out to dinner with Mom and Tom sometime in March 2010 and thinking that we were not far from needing nursing home care then. She was really very helpless at that point. I have to admit I did not say anything in March. I did not have the courage to stand up one more time to say what others did not want to hear. And that is how I contributed to the mess that followed. I went home and thought about how to find the right time to speak to Tom. Three months later, the escaping-down-the-driveway incident occurred and the hospital informed Tom that–surprise, surprise–they would not release Mom back to her home. I had fully intended to talk to Tom about making some visits to check out facilities in the area but never found the courage. In hindsight, I have learned in this and in other places in life to speak what is there to be said. My job was to advocate for my mother, who could no longer advocate for herself. Each of us has a different point of view; we must all bring our points of view to the table in order that the best decision can be made. *Don't keep silent when you see a piece no one else sees. Stand for your loved one.* Say what is in your heart, then step back from the results if you are part of a proxy team, and let the pieces fall into place. If you are advocating with a nursing home, do not stand back! Stand firm.

My speaking up might or might not have produced different results. The response to the nursing home ultimatum after Mom's wandering incident was a heroic two-day effort by my sister and Tom to find a place–at this point, any place really–to take Mom. Because they had spent no time researching nursing care options and did not understand the nature of care required for Alzheimer's disease or where Mom was in the course of it, the criteria for this now emotionally stunning decision was how to find a place in which they would feel comfortable placing her–one that looked and seemed to them the most beautiful and homey. These are usually good criteria, except that they contain no concept of the disease. Tom and my sister found a bed at a beautiful facility and put her there. It had no dementia care unit. Because she wandered, due to the normal progression of mid-stage disease she was in, she had to be put in the locked unit, which had no provisions for Alzheimer's patients. There were also no Alzheimer's-dedicated activities.

Mom, ambulatory and lovely looking, was in a top floor locked unit where she could clearly see the doors and knew she was restricted from leaving. She was there with some very frighteningly ill and mentally impaired residents. When she was escorted downstairs for activities with the other much more impaired-looking residents in wheelchairs, she could not perform the simple tasks these much less-able-looking people could. She had such difficulty reading that she could not keep up with the words to the songs, she could not play bingo and trivia: she had no answers and could not recognize the numbers. She was embarrassed and angry. I was there watching her being confused and struggling with her surroundings. At mealtime, they plopped a tray down in front of her and left her. She did not even recognize what was on her plate and did not eat half her food. I was screaming inside—for Mom, who could not scream herself. That is when I started to find my voice. Blindness and denial of the disease had created a looming crisis.

Denial creates a pattern of not seeing what is clearly there, resulting in unexpected crises calling for heroic action. When the crisis is "solved" we pat ourselves on the back for having "saved the day"! While there are many unexpected twists and turns in this disease, clear-eyed knowledge and good professional advice can help mitigate the extreme highs and lows of care-taking by helping you make informed choices. Be willing to see the disease clearly and make a well-advised care plan early on. A good professional assessment is invaluable and will help you cope with the continuing challenges of your loved one's care as well as smooth the path for them as they progress. Please see the resources listed at the end of this book!

Eventually, Mom began to act out and became agitated and uncooperative in the locked unit. One momentous day, I went to see her for a two-hour visit and was told that Mom was so uncontrollable the doctor had ordered that she be transported to the local hospital geriatric psychiatric unit for a ten-day evaluation. The ambulance was on the way.

If this sequence of events sounds familiar or has happened to you, what I have since learned is that we were in the grips of the nursing home "pattern." We had made a poor choice in our facility. The result was care that was not sufficient for Mom at that stage of her disease. This led to an agitated patient, clinical observation, and prescribed psychotropic drugs to make her malleable for the nursing home caregivers. Health-care professionals will tell you that this is standard and acceptable treatment. *It is not.* Do not be intimidated by the authority of the medical community. Listen to the unspoken messages your loved one is giving you. At every point, Mom was communicating to us what worked for her and what did not. Her agitation was her communication! Responding to the signals your loved one gives you and moving to create or find the best environment for them greatly reduces the need for psychotropic drugs. Many Alzheimer's-related authorities do not recommend their use.

Visit nursing home facilities enough to be able to tell when you are looking at peaceful, well-cared-for residents and not overly medicated patients or agitated, unhappy residents. Watch how the staff respond. At first glance, everything will seem horrible, because you are going through the trauma of placing your loved one. Get to the point where you are more familiar with different nursing home environments, allowing time for your eyes and heart to adjust accordingly so that you can see and make good decisions for your loved one!

When I got to the nursing home, Mom calmed as soon as she saw me. I removed her from the nurses' station where they were keeping her for observation and took her to her lovely room where we colored and sang and watched a beautiful red cardinal, one of her favorite birds, come and go at the bird feeder. I was so thankful for that avian angel who came to keep us company and calm my mom for me; he calmed us both.

I knew I was eventually going to have to get Mom to lie down on a gurney and be wheeled out by strangers, followed by an ambulance ride and an emergency room wait. After five and a half hours of calming, soothing, distracting activity, all she wanted to do in the emergency room was take my hand and lead the both of us out of danger—my mother always. She was finally admitted and the nurse and I tucked her into bed. She was so tired she just wanted to climb in with her clothes on. Once we got her safely in, I laid down next to her, put my arm around her, and she fell asleep while I quietly answered the admitting nurse's questions. After extracting myself from her sleeping form, I stood at the door watching her rest.

It was during this period of observation and moving her from facility to facility searching for the right fit that I wrote many of my heart-rending poems. . . .

Prayer to My Mother

You there, sleeping in the bed—
what's going on inside your head?

Where are you that we cannot see?
Oh, teach us! Teach us there to be
with you
in
marvelous fields of blue
all playful and true.

Can I come there,
stay there, with you?

Help me, help me
to pass through
so I may be there
oft, with you!

Quarry

I'm so sorry, Mom!
I'm so sorry!
There you are stuck in a rock quarry!
A quarry of life without death,
death without life.
I'm sorry, Mom, parts of your brain are gone. . .
but inside there, where it really matters,
you live behind locked doors and bars.

I'm so sorry, Mom!
You have to go so long on
hell's road to heaven.
For time long gone, untold
this drama does unfold. . . .

The drawn-out torture of night-blind sight
we seek to help—we stand outside
looking in—

And you? You know where you are!
You're here!
Right here!
And can't get through.

We love you, Mom, we really do.
I'm so sorry you have to see this through.
Another path for you I'd pick—
not keep your here like a puppet on a stick!

I love you, Mom, I really do.
Amen

Take care of your loved one by being present to reality. Make plans, understand. Do not live in denial, telling yourself this is the loving way. It is not. Face the pain early and move through it–get help and support as needed, for all of you. No one expects you to see clearly when your heart is breaking. I will talk about grief in the next chapter. If your loved one has been diagnosed with Alzheimer's, you are grieving! And your loved one *will* eventually need skilled nursing care in a nursing home or at home. It is inevitable.

Letting Go

Looking blindly at what I don't see,
emotions and thoughts seem to paralyze me.
Disconnected and drifted in parallel space,
I stop to wonder, look back, am amazed
that I see inside, in a different place,
what I must do, and where I must race
against that time and interplanetary grace
between which we float as we let go the ropes
of a loved one's life,
to release them from strife
as we set them a-sail to their next journey's place—
one we can't go to and be in that space.

Simple though it seems to open one's hand,
every sinew and muscle does not understand,
and try as we can to heed the command,
"have faith and let go"
our response is quite slow—
one worried embrace and we're tying a bow,
instead of releasing and bidding them go.

Whisper sweet words to your loved one most dear,
"My darling, I love you,
I won't hold you here."
Free in the spirit, freed in the flesh,
travel anon to that new place refreshed,

Send back your kisses, I'll catch them, my dear,
on the wings of your spirit, the song of my dreams.
I'll be with your there, you can leave me right here,
the distance is close and the space will be clear . . ."

All that's needed right now is that I understand
that it's safe and it's good
to just open my hand. . . .

For the next year we were stuck in the nursing home cycle of improperly matched care and recurring UTIs (Urinary Tract Infections) leading to agitated behaviors, all of which resulted in geriatric psychiatric observations and the over-prescribing of psychotropic medications. Mom became wheelchair-bound just after Tom and my sister moved her from her first facility into an Alzheimer's assisted-living residence. By this point her disease was too far advanced for an assisted living facility to be appropriate.* After Mom's *second* trip from there to the hospital for a UTI, we were assigned a "care" nurse to follow up with us after her stay. This kind woman recommended that for continued skilled nursing care, Mom be discharged to a rehabilitative care center close to the hospital instead of returning to assisted living. I was thrilled, as the facility she recommended had a lovely Alzheimer's unit on the upper floor.

The following poem was a reflection after we finally got Mom settled into the new place, healing from infections and the trauma of repeated hospital visits.

* *See Chapter Fifteen for comparison of different facilities.*

Encouraged

A hopeful word,
Some progress seen,
there is a glint of hope between
us all
sitting here,
circled with a loving care
'round the person we hope and dare
will soon rejoin us here and there,
as slowly back she comes
from somewhere far away she'd gone
inside one day.
With love and dedicated energy,
we've teamed and brought her back to see
the circle of us sitting here
loving her, fully and clear.

Now keep us safe going on
this scary path we tread upon,
as together, holding hands,
we work to bring about love's bands
of hope and care and clear-eyed sight
leading, guiding every day,
the joy of knowing we're on the way
to days she can live—receive, and give
life's little joys and blessings,
while we have precious time. . . .

Yet again my fellow health-care proxies were not comfortable having Mom go into the Alzheimer's unit upstairs in the rehab facility. They wanted her to recover from her bedsores first (gained during her repeated hospital visits), saying that she would not like being in the activity room with all the other residents, and feeling that the upper floor was not as attractive, and therefore as appropriate, for her. These concerns were based on observing her negative reactions to group situations at her first facility where she was unhappy with activities that were not geared to Alzheimer's patients. In *this* facility, when I took her upstairs to the Alzheimer's activity room, she had me wheel her to every table to greet everyone there. Sadly, the other proxies' perceptions were not mine, and prevailed. Mom ended up bedridden on the ground floor—in rehabilitative care—for five long months, recovering from what developed into Stage Four bedsores from her hospitalizations. With a rehabilitative staff composed of personnel with little or no dementia training, she became a forgotten patient, over-medicated and under-attended.

Worry and Toil

So sad
I'm so sad
Mom is stuck in bed
and it's real close to the end.

Sure wish it were another way
so she could enjoy some of her day
and not be sapped away
by no real chance to get up and play.

Just when we found a place to stay
that got her up on her feet
and gave her things to do,

her body says it's almost through.
Even if she has not much thought,
part of her must be bored—I'm distraught!

Helpless again to hold up that tide,
relentless unpredictableness takes its place
and drives us in its unknown race—
Against our hopes and fears prevails
its own sure course.

To no avail, our winding working
worry and toil,
exhausted in its place, gives space.

With heads bowed we sorrow and accept
no part of human effort affects
the slowing of this inexorable advent,
the leaving of the one we love
by unseen doors and windows sent
to open for their spirit's ascent.

We cannot follow there
that winding, climbing inner stair.
But bent in worry, toil here
to keep a watch upon the coil,
time-wound, as it slips away.

Only through my sister's and my vigorous determination in advocating for better treatment and attention–once the dementia care deficiencies of this last rehabilitation unit became apparent–did we start on the path that eventually led us to move Mom back to her original facility. Due to the advanced stage of her disease, Mom no longer needed to be in a locked ward there, and could now benefit from the excellent care given in another unit of that facility. She was no longer able to participate in any of the activities, and was so reduced in her awareness that she had very little concept of what was going on. Having personal interaction and kind people around her was exactly what she needed at that point. This is the challenge of nursing home care. Each situation must be custom-fitted to your loved one's needs and temperament. Only you, with your eyes wide open, can make these decisions wisely.

For Mom

Sweet sleeping Mother
gently weaving
leaping
twining
meshing
melding
pining . . .
May your days be filled with dreams—
places where the mind still seems
itself
intact
in whole
in fact—
part
of who you are. . . .

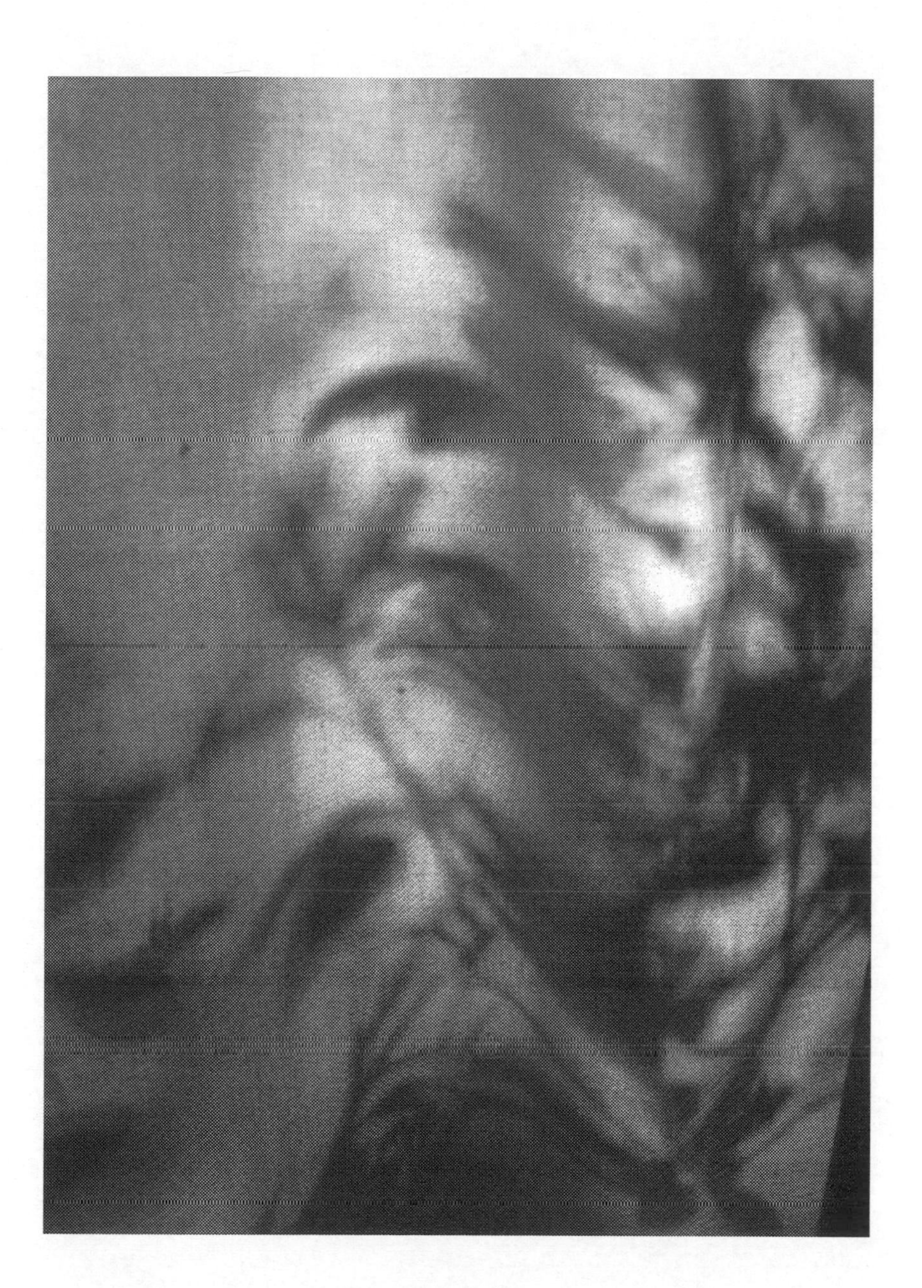

Shadows VI

Chapter Eight

Fear: Ours, His and Hers

Bless her, oh Lord, with a peep of what's true. . . .

When I write, I write in longhand, in colors that express my thoughts and emotions. I had to switch colors to write this chapter. Interestingly enough, I wrote it in green, the color of hope and healing.

What is fear? According to one dictionary: "a distressing emotion aroused by impending danger; something that causes a feeling of dread or apprehension."

For my sister and me, fear was not knowing. We have kissed our grandmother goodbye to Alzheimer's and watched as all of her four daughters have succumbed to this irreparable disease. And we, my sister and I, are the next generation.

Our fear is not knowing–not knowing what is buried within each of our genetic make-ups. What has been passed on and not passed on? What triggers and what heals? Will one of us get it and not the other? Which one? Is it avoidable? What can we do? What does the medical community know, not know? Will there be a cure? Will it be in time?

In Tom's case, his was the fear of not doing enough, of missing something, and of what came next in this awful journey. Fear of the nursing home, fear of pain and suffering he could not divert, fear of the end he could not allay with all his love and care, fear of not being enough.

And Mom? My beautiful mother? She feared what she knew. Hers was the fear of death, of coming to the end, of going to that place from which she would not return to any of what she had previously known—that new place to which we all go. . . .

Fear of The Next

The joy of reading what I wrote
is sometimes more powerful than a word of hope.
It lifts my spirit just to hear
words I wrote when I was clear . . .

Not muddled like now,
caught in worry's cloud,
suspended somewhere in between
what's life and earth and what's unseen—

New future's changing face and dream,
of choices not to be concurred,
results we wish to not incur,
places we would rather not be—
roads and possibilities. . . .

They all converge, one ball of twine
past that horizon we cannot find,
out there somewhere beyond our scope.
We only wish and pray and hope
we have the depth and strength to cope,
the courage found, to meet the challenge;
the grace to persevere and manage
the winding hidden path that leads
to where we do not know at last. . . .

Oh, let me read those words again—
the ones where we were laughing!
Let me hold your hand and look back then,
remembering you, my mother, my friend.

That fall, before we left on vacation for two weeks, I had a conversation with Mom. I spoke as if she had no disease at all. I conversed with her about life, about death, and about dying. I told her that we loved her and wanted her to know it was all right to go, to leave, if she needed to, while we were gone. That we would be okay–she did not need to stay for us. I wanted to make sure that if something happened while we were away she would know it was okay to leave us. She looked up at me, and in her few labored words said, "I am afraid."

My heart tore, and I wept. To be inching inexorably away from us, up to the edge of The Next, with great fear, is hell here on earth. It makes dying from Alzheimer's a great, drawn-out torture. When you are faced with your death or the death of a loved one over an extended period of time, somehow, somewhere, it needs to become your friend.

After church the next Sunday before we left, my husband and I brought communion to Mom. We used a beautiful new traveling communion set just blessed for use that morning. I brought my Bible and a hymnal. I went online and found the words to the hymn, "Be Not Afraid." Mom reached eagerly and knowingly for both the cup and the bread. As life would have it, soon after this she was no longer able to eat anything other than ground or pureed foods, and our parting gift of communion was perfectly timed. What a precious gift that I am so glad we were able to give!

After that, I simply prayed. I knew that Spirit works slowly and gently. I prayed for her dreams, that she might resolve her fears in them and that they might bring her close to those beautiful ones waiting to greet her; that she would be beautiful and strong and ready in her spirit when her time came; that she would slip the knots of earthly shore and sail peacefully, serenely, confidently away on her chosen day.

Nothing but Fear
it's nothing but Fear
that keeps us Here
instead of There.

Nothing but Fear
it's nothing but Fear
that keeps us hovering here
instead of stretching wings afar.

We shiver and delay, say courage can wait
for another day,
just let me think a little while more . . .

while it's nothing but Fear
nothing but Fear
that keeps us here evermore.

We can toss it aside
take one step and glide
the rest of the way through
Our courage will come out, and walk with us, too.

Oh, it's nothing but Fear
nothing but Fear
that keeps us hovering here.

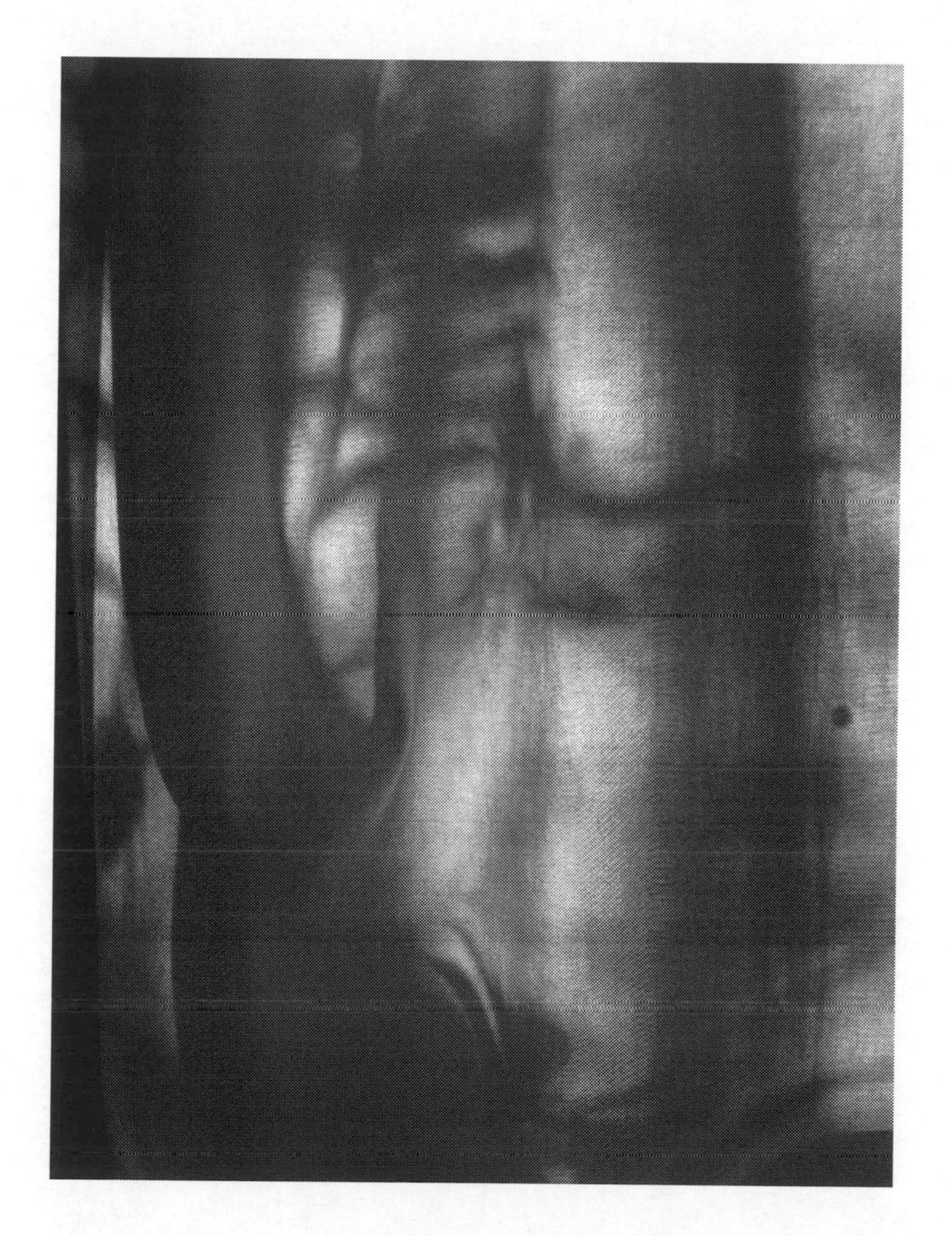

Shadows VII

Chapter Nine

Grief

No more tears, no more tears,
No more tears left to cry. . . .

Grief is a constant companion to this disease. It spreads its aura over, in, about and through us all as we *must* go down this path.

In Alzheimer's disease, grief precedes death; it is a long, slow process of inching loss upon loss, each new facet bringing its own renewed sense of bereavement, powerlessness and angst.

Wikipedia.com defines grief as "a multi-faceted response to loss." I want you to know that I wrote the word "love" after the word "loss" in this definition when I first wrote it out, and so my definition became "a multi-faceted response to the loss of love." The definition goes on to say "particularly to the loss of something or someone to whom a bond was formed [love!]. Although conventionally focused on emotional response to loss," it says, "grief also has physical, cognitive, behavioral, social and philosophical dimensions. . . . Bereavement refers to the state of loss, and grief is the reaction to loss."

Profound

She's profoundly impaired.
I am profoundly sad.
Tears cannot a grief express,
not this one
that goes on and on.
It runs and trickles underground
unseen in its paths.
When we surface to face its pain
we've lost our footing again . . .
I am immobilized, sodden,
dragging unseen burdens
cast behind me so I will not see
the crashing, staring emptying
of what is to be.

There is no place of refuge,
no hope to be free . . .
I limp and linger here and stop
and feel its weight, see its
looming horror shape,

cast it firmly behind my back
and trudge on. . . .

Further along in the definition, Wikipedia starts to use the term "loss" interchangeably with the word "death." In Alzheimer's disease, they are not the same. Loss occurs from the moment the disease is perceived. Grief is a close companion from that point on. You walk with it constantly, hate it, refuse it, fight it, talk with it and eventually hold hands with it, as you go down the path drawn for you by the slow-moving, unpredictable losses of your loved one's disease.

There is no map, no chart.

No other person's experiences will help you to map your own.

It's you and Grief going on together.

Welcome to the family of loss . . . and pain . . . and something gained. . . .

In an article entitled "The Poet Within–Easing the Pain of Change" by Cheryl Perrault, she described my journey with my mother as being one of "going deep within myself . . . to root out and heal dark places and bring myself into joy". . . and, as poetry has been my chosen means of expression she said: "We can put into poetry what would otherwise annihilate our souls–and make it beautiful."

Grief is the emotion experienced over any loss in life. It is best that we make friends with it early and soon. Broken-heartedness will not destroy a soul, but resisting it will.

The Pain of Death

So sad.
My nose is red!
My eyes are dry.
I've had myself
a good big cry.

All better soon, I sang to her.
Soon it will be better.
All will be free
without life's fetter.

here in earth's bright sphere,
the weight too much to bear,
soon the weather will be clear,
and you, no longer here,
will ne'er be far away!

Like the breath of the air,
sung on a prayer,
the tether cut, the rope is freed,
you'll wing your way with all Godspeed.

And silver, silken-like you'll be,
sweet soft whisper's mystery,
my mother angel always.

One of the gifts of walking with grief every day was learning to work with my sister a little more closely and humanly. Mom's biggest lament as we grew up and apart was that she would like to put us in a bowl and mix us up—and have, as I supposed, the perfect child. Mom used to say that eventually, one day, there would be just us two sisters, walking together, and that we'd better learn how.

To My Sister

Peaceful,
I am peaceful now.

At rest because,
after all this time,
we have finally begun.
You heard me, saw me,
I saw you.
We both have shuddered over what is done.

In accord we understand,
can go forward hand in hand,
giving and receiving life's commands.

Mom has done it, all she can.
She made us work and think and plan,
communicate and understand:
gift of life, from her own hand. . . .

Grief, while it feels isolating, brings us together in our humanity, our mortality. We lose life's differences in the face of any great loss, and find its commonalities.

Why?

Why is it so hard for us to understand?
What looks like death to us
is just a plan—

an order to the universe,
a scheduled metamorphosis.

Just ask any caterpillars
spinning their cocoons—
you think they know
they'll be butterflies soon?

In some built-in ritual of faith they spin
their sepulcher, and then go in.

To them it's the end;
to us begins
the flight of monarchs,
spiraled arcs
of color,
a fairy's flight for our delight!

They feed upon the nectar bright and swing high away
into light.

Poor little caterpillar here in its cocoon
has nestled into death and doom . . .

It all depends on where you stand,
how you see,
what you know,
and faith's bright glow. . . .

Shadows VIII

Chapter Ten

On Death and Life

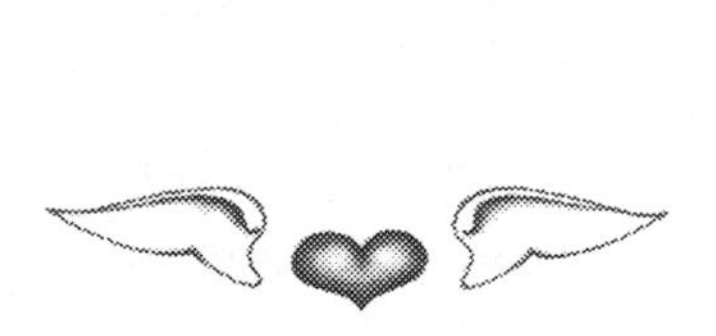

On death . . .

I know you thought that a chapter on grief was enough, and that now I would lighten in tone. I must go here first; stay with me.

Alzheimer's changes your perspective on life and death. Death is what you have while you are living with Alzheimer's. It is not a single event; it is the daily depletions and losses—the living mortality of its pain.

The final act of dying is the end of death.

All this would sound very glum and tragic if we failed to understand that life is happening at the same time. That is the wonder of our humanness. Only in this dimension—of time or whatever you choose to call it—here on earth, do we experience both life and death together.

Look Up!

Look up! Into pine-wooded hills,
Sunlight dappled, oh! What a thrill!

Look down!
Deep into silent, waiting ground. . .

Death, it scares us,
seems to tear us.

From our birth
our shells belong to Mother Earth;
we cycle back organic matter
deep in every molecule—
earth calls us to remember
and be part of
one with
all we are.

Down below, this silent star
holds the key to what will be
the next generation's start—
deep rooted, in her heart.

On life . . .

The greater question here might really be: What is life?

And I think, after having watched, listened and walked through this process of daily dying, I am more appreciative of–and sensitive to–what I perceive as life.

Technically speaking, air in the lungs and a beating heart signify physical life. When those stop, we are physically dead. In between this black-and-white of death and life is living, and "alive-ing"–that place of breathing existence without conscious awareness or joy. I wrote this next poem in agony, going through the horrible advances of the disease we were powerless to stop, and grappling with our own confusions over how to deal with them.

Worse than Dying

Worse than dying
is alive-ing
when the rest of you is gone
and someone in their fear and pain
wants to keep you from moving on.

Worse than dying
is all the trying
we do to put it off—

that leaving, ending, crying part
where we all live in fear,

that crying, ending, dying part,
when we're no longer here.

Worse than dying
is alive-ing
when there's no place to be.
Worse than dying is alive-ing
trapped and caught,
unfree.

In a withered body-mind
a spirit cannot be!

Bond-held,
trapped back
from eternity.

Worse than dying
is alive-ing
not allowing to be seen
the truth of living spirit
bound in flesh so we can be

consoled and comforted
by someone else's life
even when they truly are
no longer alive.

Moving, moving, moving. . . .

That is what life on this planet, in this space and time, always brings us to.

The beauty and joy of this earth–even here in the midst of Alzheimer's disease with its pain and trials–is evident. We so often ask, "Why? Why all this beauty and pain, joy and death?"

Where Do Butterflies Go When They Die?

And why,
why, oh why
do they fly?
Wouldn't it be better if they never tried?
All that energy spent—
and for what? And why?

We waste our time when we try
to frame a life upon a parchment plain.
No piece is ever isolated, free
but flows with some magnetic harmony
in scenes as yet we cannot see.

So lift and power off with me
the beauty of transformity
the power, light and soul to free
to truly see and truly be
the wings of life's eternity.

Life: our affirmation of hope.

The Journey

Chapter Eleven

Lessons of the Journey

Oh, to swoop—an effortless glide
from near to far, and not be over-wide
or stretched beyond our par,
when view we from infinite perspective
see the whole, the minute, with clarity's perfection . . .

On these pages I share with you the joys and connections I found, as well as the deep pains and truths I wrestled with on my journey through Alzheimer's disease with my mother. They are expressed through the poetic words of my heart as we slogged our way through the horror of five months of bed rest ordered by the doctor. I moved through the pain of this challenging time to a new place of rest and acceptance through my writing.

I invite you to join me in the stages of my caregiving experience with Alzheimer's: Coping, Accepting, Remembering, Finding Little Joys, Creating Moments, Resolving.

Coping:

Gloomy Thoughts on a Rainy Day

Slog the marshy bands of fog
fair pluming with its rain
pelting on the windowpane.
Gray is just amorphous in its wash,
color and perspective lost—
in clear relief a stalking trunk or piercing points of pine,
nothing is quite kind
but somber, soft,
of muted cloth
a climbing road entwined
a misty wood, dripping on for miles
it rides—
I sigh with gloom and glum
to watch a day so done. . . .

I'm gray like the weather
hung in time by a tether
stuck on a second like a pin,
waiting for the next to begin.

A long, drawn-out breath,
never reaching the end,
a floating sigh
a chain of lights
swift-moving through oncoming night
never-ending, winding there
like some undulating, ethereal stair.
hanging time and energy here.

Beware:
we cannot simply live
eternally unaware,
forestalling the end in fear,
O breathe us in and out—
expel us utterly
and be gone,
long-waiting dread of a thing not done.

Blow us out and along
to be over, or begun—

it does not matter.
They are one.

Accepting:

Patience

She lies upon the bed so weak,
supine and gentle.
I want to knock softly
to see if she is there and will come out to meet me:

a shadow self
upon a pillow shelf.

They lift and turn and feed and care,
they speak in whispers when they are there.

I sing and draw and stroke her hair.

Oh, person who is barely there!
She smiles upon her comfort stretched—
unable even to support her weight.
so patient she has become—
I understand now,
She's waiting for things to get done. . . .
Gently, and with good grace,
knowing she is not in charge,
that discomfort is a state to be born,
like pleasure, in its time.

I think, I feel, begin to understand,
and hope for her
that time has worked its cure
upon her soul and mind,

that, patient and forgiving,
gentle and kind,
her spirit strengthened, ready to find
the balm and solace for which it has yearned.

A peacefulness has climbed into our journey.
A loving, gentle care, one of just being there . . . to love
and sing and pray, wait with her patiently
for what is not there. . . .

Oh, give us too this graciousness
to bow our heads and bend our breasts
upon the waiting time to be.
Let us deliver patiently
the fire-tried soul
refined, though battered,
as if the heart is all that mattered. . . .

Gems

The colors of life are seldom seen
except through trouble's heightening sheen.

Yet they glow with richness, softness, truth
and deepening beauty as we gaze.

Reach out and look, don't turn away;
what's pain today
becomes
the colors of the tapestry,
rich jewel-tones of life—
see beauty in each strife.

Light a candle.
Get quiet.
Dig deep with your thoughts.
Let go and follow
the peace of your heart.

Remembering:

Memories

I miss your memories . . .
the ones you had of me, of us,
the validation of your knowing me.
You held my history,
now part of it's forgotten,
lost to both of us—
the part you knew.

Who else remembered
how I learned to tie my shoe?
My favorite foods, special doll,
my childhood struggles to understand it all?

You held my space—
I didn't know
until you had to let it go,
how much it meant to have you there
standing in my past
with loving care.
Thanks for all those years
you held my trust
and kept my history in place.

I'll anchor now for my own children grown
their truth in time and space.

Stay or Go

Time is a rushing tide,
it does take things away.

We hold for but a little while
till on its waves we race.

Hold fast, or let it go
the choice is made
by us, or for us, on every tide.

Lose some past, a future to make
And always while here, we've been—
we are—choosing
somewhere unseen, to stay or go, each hour, each day
till those tides of time roll us away.

Are we caught, or freed by its speed?
You say. It's your day. . . .

Finding Little Joys:

On good days we would play, she following me with her eyes from the bed–watching me blow bubbles, singing or reading, she holding her stuffed dog . . . a beautiful soft memory she could feel.

One day I sat and wrote poems for her. This first is about the little stuffed dog she had.

Doggy soft upon my bed
sitting close to my head
soft and warm and gentle there

you watch over me with all your care,
sweet, my doggy, sitting there. . . .

And of her favorite jacket with the lighthouses on it:

Lighthouses in the night!
Guarding over us with their light
'round us, keep us, ever bright
never far from God's sight. . . .

I would often be there when she ate her meals. It was so amazing to watch the woman who sternly taught me to eat all my peas and carrots become the delighted dessert-eater in advance. She clearly went first for whatever food gave her the most joy. And I—well, a little gentle prodding— but what are you going to do? This is my mother, and she is dying. "Enjoy your dessert!"

Lessons from Mom

Eat all the sweet stuff first.
It is good.
The rest will still be food.
Say what you want.
Shout NO! when you mean it.
Hold your ground.
Honor your space.
Think very carefully.
In everything you do,
be very deliberate,
and don't forget to chew.

Peach Pie!

Oh my, peach pie!
Bite off more than you can chew!
Oh my! Peach pie,
delightful, for you.
Sweet and gold,
soft crust, too.
Peach pie sweet—
and I sit,
watching you. . . .

Creating Moments:

Since my mother was the product of a very English background, afternoon tea was a special time in our house. To be shut in a nursing home with only washed-out tea bags and plastic cups full of chlorine-tasting water and mini-cups of preservative-laden cream substitute is not proper *Tea*. So, occasionally we had:

A Cup of Tea

A cup of tea
I bring to thee
to share in a room so drear.
Soft-spoken whisper of many a time
you held it, drew it near
with steadier hand and eyes that were clear. . . .
Yet even now your memory sounds
as if to signal here:
it is to taste and drink and remember.

You softly turn the cup
and from life's contemplation
sometimes you look up
and see me, standing there
hoping I have touched you here
in some profound ritual of the ordinary cup—
a yearning for your remembering
of a daughter's love.

I was determined to help Mom observe Christmas, a celebration she loved, by creating stamped bookmarks for the staff.

Regrets

We made them together,
those bookmarks,
you and I.
Me pressing the little wooden block you held,
shaking and jerking,
in an unsteady, dropping grasp,
urging you with my mind not to let go
so that we could make one impression together
upon a little piece of paper—
a flimsy, fragile thing.

I'd never seen anyone shake so much
trying to put a hand in a place.
The whole concentration of your effort
as you tried to work with me
inspired awe at your determination,
terrified me of your helplessness.

There! We made one!
One impression in time.

And then you would unerringly
raise the red-stained wooden block to your mouth
for a taste.
Laughable, and horrifying.

How do I, the child, tell my mother no?
How do we, the bound, let each other go?

And, like the winds of time and the rushing tides, it was January, a New Year, and the month of her birth. . . .

Happy Birthday!

May the winds of time
waft gently through your hair
and bring my love and thoughts
to you on every breath of air.
May love surround you every day
through everyone
who comes your way.

God keep you safe, secure and warm
wrapped in love through every storm.

May heaven's light shine in your soul,
guard and keep you ever whole.

And so through these dark days of rushing, cold-bearing fall into the long nights of winter we watched bedside with Mom as she, oh so slowly, healed from her bedsores. . . . And something else was healed as we did.

Oh, Mom!

Oh, Mom, sometimes for thee I cry.
Sometimes for thee I sigh.

A laugh, a sorrow,
a joy, a gain—
to be with you brings love and pain.

Thank you for listening
to my poetry,
for leaving open the page
and placing the book near.

For in your labored,
missing mind
not missing me here.
I've learned to love you more
the more I touch your soul.
It looks at me through eyes of love
that always were right there.
I only saw them stare
in disapproval
and missed the love that
passed beneath—
I never saw it
till I came to you with love,

looked for you in time,
and was content to be the child
you knew I am inside.

Resolving: the End of This Part of Our Journey

After a long and debilitating spell in the rehab center we moved Mom back to her first facility: a beautiful place where she was well cared for, but which did not have the Alzheimer's offerings she had so desperately needed before.

Mom herself was the guiding force in this move. As she healed, she became more and more combative towards the rehab center staff, initiating a doctor-ordered visit to the local hospital's geriatric psychiatric unit. She was not combative there. When the doctor ordered a second geriatric psychiatric visit to a different hospital, once again Mom was complacent and happy. My sister and I realized it was time to move her.

Due to the advanced stage of her disease, Mom felt at home and was well cared for in an unsecured wing of her first facility. As it was late summer when we moved her, we would take walks, me pushing her wheelchair outside to one of the lovely garden areas, where sometimes she would just peacefully fall asleep. . . .

In the Garden

Napping in the Garden of Eden
soft water lapping
sweet breezes laden
with flowers and nectar
the gods of the hours do meet thee there—
where, on a whisper, you dare to dream.

Napping in the Garden of Eden, you seem
transported on an angel's breath
deep down into
God's own depths
to splash and play
and laugh your way
from here to there
without a care
in the Garden of Eden—
where you now dare
to roam and know
no matter how far you go,
you're home.

What Is the Soul?

What is the soul—
a thing that
knows the whole?

But is it me,
my personality,
or that which connects us all together?

Once your loved one is peaceful and well cared for, and you have a sense of having landed in the right spot, there is a welcome pause, a breathing space, for you both. Alzheimer's is a capricious disease: like a zephyr in the field, it blows this way and that, unannounced, carrying you with it. A small resting space is a welcome respite, and I was grateful for this one.

Come float with me on inner air . . . spiraling up and downward there. . . .

Thank you for for joining me in this part of the journey!

Shadows IX

Chapter Twelve

Memories

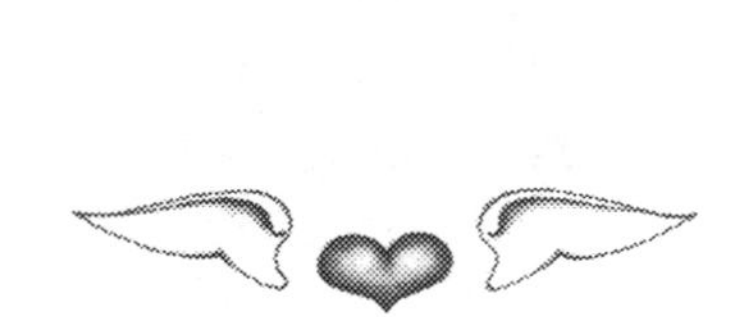

A Call to My Sister

Don't you sometimes wish you could just talk to Mom?
Tell her you love her,
see how it's going?
Chew the fat as in days of old
when you didn't know what you had was pure gold?

Remember those long lazy afternoon talks,
the tears and the hopes and the way that she spoke
words of wisdom and comfort and love,
even sometimes giving a push or a shove?

When you needed reinforcement she was there—
protective as a mother bear in her remote care
of our lives.

A solace in every storm, you could count on her.
She'd roll up her sleeves and jump in
when the pot got too warm

and you needed an extra hand
just to help you stand
steady.

Don't you wish you could just pick up the phone,
say, "Hi Mom, love you.
How you doin'?"

In this chapter you will hear the voice of my mother, a prolific writer and poet in her time, and the voices of her granddaughters.

Mom listened as I told her about this book. When I asked her if she wanted me to publish some of her writing in it, she looked at me, and, very slowly, as I waited and watched, she delved back into the storehouse of her mind, found the word she was looking for, brought it forward, and commanded her mouth to form the word "files." Oh joy! A gift! She had sent me to her files!

At her house not an hour later I found in her files a treasure trove of love, self-expression and memories. I'd like you to meet Barbara Lee Durling Goepel Shibles Miller. This is her poetry.

I know the pang of loneliness
when all the work is done,
the searing pain of loss
that comes
with the setting of the sun.

The struggle to get up each day
to face another dawn
when your greatest motivation
is not there to cheer you on!

Now is the time where comfort comes
from friends and family dear,
But take your burden to the Lord
who's always there to hear.

He loves you and will heal your heart
if you will keep him near.

Written for Chuck C. on the passing of his dear wife, Peggy
—July 2000

My body is weary and tired, Lord,
I know not which way to turn.
My mind is a mass of confusion;
My eyes in their sockets burn.

You promised my burden you'd share
If I your yoke would willingly wear;
My spirit I turn over to thee, Lord,
To refresh, refuel and repair.

The dangers within far exceed, I fear,
the hazards that lay in my way,
Only Jesus can strengthen and brighten
my poor aching soul today.

—Circa 1985

High above the mountains
Storm clouds run.
Billowing gray darkens the sun.
Strong winds and cold
Blow over the sea,
Icy fingers of fear
Are clutching at me.

Oh God of creation!
Reach down in your Love—
Remind me the sun
Is still shining above!
No matter the storm
That surrounds me today,
Your love and your strength
Will show me the way.

—January 1998

Lost in April

Golden-haired April—
Flouncing your saucy green petticoats,
Glancing with your azure eyes
Through the filmy gray mantle
That hovers over
Your swelling loveliness—

Sometimes hiding your
Breathless promise
Under a lowering brow
While great cascades of tears
Obscure your quickening beauty.
Then, as the capricious breeze
Ruffles your shawl,
Once again your radiant smile
Lifts my soul and leaves me breathless,
Wondering and impatient for your next surprise.

Charlotte Hunt (pen name)
—April 1977

You have a lovely garden.
Each day, as I drive by,
I quickly check for blossoms new
From the corner of my eye.
If by chance a traffic jam
Should slow me to a crawl,
Then what a happy chance I have
To see those blossoms all!

A poem of thanks to the people whose beautiful
perennial garden I pass on my way to work each day
—Summer of '91

If I can cheer a weary heart
Or make a sad face smile;
If I can lend a willing ear
And listen for a while;
If I can ease a heavy load
Along my busy way;
Then Lord, I thank you for the grace
You've given me today.

Barbara Durling Goepel Shibles
—May 19, 1999

It's Monday morning;
There's work to do:
I've got to rinse out
A thought or two.
There's a lingering doubt
that needs a scrub;
A hamper of worries
To dump in the tub.
A hasty word
Needs a dose of bleach;
An unkind thought
Must be stored beyond reach.
Monday's work doesn't end
With the setting sun,
Tuesday will bring
New tasks to be done.

Charlotte Hunt (pen name)
—Autumn 1977

Night Notes

So many hearts to mend—
Mend mine
So many wills to bend—
Bend mine
So many burdens to share—
Share mine
So many griefs to bear—
Bear mine
So many paths to pave—
Pave mine
So many souls to save—
Save mine!

—Circa 1988

A Monday in May

Some time to myself
To think and pray
To plan, to enjoy
This beautiful day;
To read Sunday's papers
And linger
In the misty golden morning.
Some time to myself
To sit in the sun
To watch gray squirrels

Circle and run;
To see tiny leaves
Unfolding
Against an azure sky.

Oh, thank you, God,
For Life and Spring
both eternally renewed.

—Spring 1984

What a precious look into my mother's soul her writings have afforded me! Parts of herself she was reticent to share are here for the beautiful nourishment only a mother can give.

I have laughed and cried, been provoked and sighed over the passages and stories she has left me. So many memories wrapped in time's precious gift of words. Thank you, Mom!

She wrote hilarious tales of our sailboat sails, odes and diatribes to events and happenings of her time. She wrote about the inspirations and soul-revelations of her life. They are all here, meticulously typed out on yellowed sheets of diaphanous paper, small imprints of her soul, the pages holding the memory of her hands, the concentration of her labors and emotions. They are a spiritual experience to go through. Thank you for reading some of them with me.

About six months after Mom went into the nursing home, I knew she was really going away from us quickly and sent the SOS around to my children. All my daughters lived on the other side of the country and could not get back to see their grandmother or say goodbye. I told them that if they had anything to say to their grandmother, to write it and send it to me now, that I would read their words and thoughts and feelings to their grandmother while she could still hear and understand them.

There is a story about a king who had a rich treasure chest full of beautiful, priceless treasures. He kept it locked away, but whenever his children were about he would unlock it and open it, and share all his rich treasures with his children. Many years passed, and his children spent many wonderful times with their father going through the beautiful treasures in his treasure chest. Finally, the children all grew up and went away, and the king became older and older, and alone, and sick. When the children came back to visit, they found their father's treasure chest empty. All the beautiful treasures they had shared together were gone. The children then began to bring their own treasures with them when they visited, and slowly filled up the empty chest with the memories and treasures of their youth. The king was rich once again, with all the treasures of his children. This is the story of Alzheimer's. Below are some of the treasures my mother's granddaughters brought to refill her treasure chest of memories and experiences.

Here are their letters, their memories of their grandmother, their thanks for her in their lives.

Grandma,

I love you so much. I want to thank you for always being my champion and I want you to know that I am really okay now. You are a beautiful woman and person and I am proud that you are my Grandma.

Love, Heide

Please tell Grandma THANK YOU . . .

Thank you for fresh blueberry pancakes and fresh salads, grown with love and picked with care.

Thank you for giving me the joy of reading, you sat at the end of our beds and took us away into another world, you read out loud to us . . . emphasizing words and using tone and volume to really allow me to feel like I was in the story. I have read that way ever since.

When I got a little older, you offered me a new comfort . . . Reader's Digest, and a quiet place to lose myself in stories. I learned that solitude, silence and "me time" was very important. I still make time for myself to this day.

Thank you for showing me the importance of beauty, thank you for holidays where I knew I was special, thank you for summers of going to the beach, rowing in the dinghy, catching crabs at low tide, feeding the ducks, my first experience with sewing—you taught me how to be vibrant at any age by doing cartwheels on the front lawn, riding bikes with me and swimming for fun, exercise and relaxation—you taught me that I can hold someone to a high standard and still make them feel like the most important, special, loved person they are. I never felt anything but love from you. You never kissed me quietly, you grabbed my face, puckered up and made a loud,"MMMAAAAA" sound. You were not just kissing me, you were telling me and everyone around just how much you loved me.

Thank you Grandma . . .

I love you,
Ingrid

Hi Grandma,

You may not fully remember me at this point but I remember lots about you. I am so thankful we spent time together when I was a little girl. The memories I made at that age will stick with me even now.

I remember the festive parties at your house—you have a wonderful way of welcoming people into your home and giving time and attention to their comfort. You are the best hostess! The Halloween parties stand out as one of my most vivid childhood memories. The basement was set up for the kids and decorated like it was from another world. There was punch and sweets but the games were always the best part! You started this family tradition and I am happy to continue to pass it on to my kids one day.

I am so thankful that I will forever get to carry a little piece of you around in me where ever I go. Thank you for being my grandmother. I miss you often and love you so much. I have the perfect photo of you from my wedding, smiling from ear to ear while dancing the night away with Tom. This is how I will always remember you. I wish I could wrap my arms around you and give you a hug and a kiss goodbye.

I love you Grandma,
Jenny

Jennifer also described her grandmother as choosing to have great experiences to share with her grandchildren–a particularly poignant comment from a grown grandchild, and a tribute to Mom's dedicated delight in creating her relationship with them.

My youngest daughter wrote a beautiful note to her "Dear Sweet Grandma" in which she recalled coming to visit for the weekends when she was young, and how special it was to have that alone time with her grandmother. They played games and made crafts, and Mom introduced her to wonderful movies such as *Hans Christian Anderson* and *The Journey of Natty Gann*. They loved combing the Cape Cod beaches together and made jewelry from the seashell treasures they found. Mom's keepsakes and old photos of a different time and era fascinated her. Most of all, she felt a deep connection to Mom through their shared love of music; she felt music was a living memory of her grandmother and that as a singer, her voice is a part of her grandmother that she will always have with her and can pass on to others. When she made a trip East to see Mom before this, my daughter gently sang to her grandmother and sensed the wonderful connection that music makes with a loved one with Alzheimer's. In that poignant moment, music brought them together for a brief–but true–flash of recognition.

What an amazing and precious experience to be able to see my mother through the eyes and hearts of my daughters! I saw her plucky fun-spiritedness, her deep caring and nurturing. I saw her passing on traditions and teaching values. I saw her appreciated and revered for who she was and the many blessings she imparted to my children's lives. I am privileged to have had this little peep into their relationships–these other mirrors in which to see my mother across the generations. Thanks, Mom, for showing me your heart in so many different ways.

I hope you have enjoyed these memories of a very human life–a vulnerable soul who passed this way and managed to spread love and wisdom while wrestling with the challenges, disappointments and fears of her own life.

Mom's story is the story of many. As you walk through the solemn, quiet rooms of a nursing home and watch the muted vacant faces of its dementia residents, know that each one of them holds the rich treasure of a life fully lived, now tucked deep within their spheres of existence and being. They are consummately worthy of infinite care, respect and love as they live their final days with us here.

A World Without Alzheimer's

Oh the bliss!
To think of it makes me almost miss
the heartache of each dawn that breaks
across an increasingly vacant face
to fall upon the silent caregiver watching there

Is this a good day or a bad?

Until we arrive at that wondrous shore
where memory does not recede upon the tide
Please welcome all who come
with lost places and blind minds
into your hearts and world

They long to taste its moments once more
Your acceptance is a gift most rare
Your understanding of how to greet them with care
is like fine jewelry they can wear
with dignity and pride

Your knowing that they live inside
beyond that place where we can see
beyond the reach of memory
in Now – right Here -with Us

Aunt Shirley, Grandmother Daisy holding Mom
(two years old)
1925

The Durlings
Grandfather Arthur, Aunt Shirley, twins Jean and Joan, Mom, Grandmother Daisy

Mom and Dad's wedding, 1945
Grandmother Daisy in between Mom and Dad

Mom and Dad circa 1955

Thanksgiving 1954
Mom is third from left.

Still sailing and swimming!
circa 2003

Four generations: Grandmother Daisy,
me, Mom, Heide and Ingrid, 1975

Mom and Tom circa 2003

Passage

Chapter Thirteen

Saying Goodbye

I have said so many goodbyes.
I have had so many good cries.
And always another comes by,
A place within, where deeply, I sigh
And begin again to let go . . .

Love is holding loosely, they say.

And so it is, every day, a question of allowing your loved one to go to where the disease is taking him or her. Alzheimer's is not a disease of fight and battle—while science has found medications to slow its apparent symptoms, there is, as yet, no cure and no reversal possible.

There is only coping, and learning, and loving, and leaving.

The biggest challenges are to learn to read your loved one's behaviors and expressions, and to respond to those needs in ways that keep both of your lives as healthy, calm and connected as possible. You will need to exercise the emotional muscles of acceptance and love, while keeping a sharp eye out for that always unexpected, uncharted next step. Then you must learn how to cope and love in the new place to which the disease has brought you.

Sad

I'm used to being sad
even when I'm glad.
Don't know if that's bad
but oh! It makes me sad—
to come to clearing space and know
I have sadness like a cancer grown
to live with when I live alone
with my thoughts and feelings shown.

My sorrow lingers like a mist
overcoming shapes and forms
settling in the hollows of my soul.
Its soft coolness follows me where're I go
and spreads about me places others cannot enter in,
a solemnity they do not care to see,
but falter when they have perceived.

I wonder how long I'll be in this eternity
of waiting for an ending not yet seen,
holding her hand
rubbing her head
saying "I love you" to her fading mind
kissing time and space farewell
but never letting go.

She clings, a weak thing,
tendrils of love reaching out to me
when I sing to her,

eyes that try to speak words I cannot always hear.
I wonder how much longer we will be
caught in this sad, soft place
before eternity. . . .

Once you understand and accept who is in charge here—which is neither you nor your loved one—your journey becomes a little easier. Fighting the reality of Alzheimer's disease will wear you out, down and thin, very quickly.

I said goodbye to my mother so many times, in so many ways—and yet I think that more deeply, it was the desire say goodbye to the disease that tore and shredded my heartstrings. Here are the poems that express the wandering journeys of my heart, where I held for Mom that space of victory she ultimately achieved, and where I learned to say my own goodbyes.

Where is my mother going?
Where, do you believe?
Who is really leaving?
What do you perceive,
when, standing by the side of death,
you see?

Tears . . .

No more tears,
no more tears,
no more tears left to cry

No more ways,
no more ways,
no more ways to say goodbye

No more days,
no more days,
no more days left to try

Memories,
memories softly lie . . .

Keep your peace!
Hush you still, deep inside.
Go in grace, beauty's eye

No more tears,
no more tears,
dry your eyes

Softly go
softly peace
soft you fly

Gentle wings
freedom brings
as we die.

Lay you down,
let you go
do not try

We'll be here,
we'll be fine
we're alive

Leave us now,
let us go—
we will make it,
that you know—

Kiss us here
dry our tears,
wave farewell

Soft away
don't you stay!
We're okay, love you well!

Look! I see;
you float free
happy, young, and well

Waft away,
do not stay . . .
take the wind and ride away

No more tears
no more fears
left to stay . . .

No more tears
no more fears
time or years.

Mom

Soon,
you will see everything true—
this is just a long dark tunnel you are going through.

Transition, birth,
as you leave the earth you will all see—
the stars, the light, the energy.

Hang tight!
Being re-born is new flight
as souls, unseen here, become their sight.
For some, death is easy, scheduled, and nice;
for others, a long fight, a difficult path
to leave the earth,
tight-held.

At last,
Heaven opens with a blast!

Light! Love! and Energy abound!
Healed, with Life all around!
Time to leave, let go,
say goodbye—
as you, freed and marvelous, fly.

Resounding with energy and light
fill us here with your new sight,
send us back a crumb or two,
that we, in memory, may share with you!

Rise! Arise! and take your place
in beautiful memory, energy and space!

It's so hard to say goodbye, and yet, it can be a welcome relief. In fact, there are times that you look for it and long for it, just so you know that your loved one is free.

New Beginnings

Clean the slate!
Off life's freight!
Woe and tears unlaid
bare upon the docks of time,
its price is fully paid.

Soft drop that load right here
its passage paid in tears,
unburdened by our ills and fears,
our ticket suddenly appears!

Reach out your hand and take it now,
the full fare paid for you,
glide gently through the last toll booth,
and looking forward, smile.

Don't even turn once more around,
we're fine, our feet are on the ground;
sail right through, heaven's new child,
soft with grace and fully wild.

The final chapters of this book will walk you through what I trust you will find as some very practical, soothing and hope-engendering steps. I am giving you the facts and information I found most helpful and supportive to me as I struggled with my daily realities and anxieties, along with suggestions for both living with and being present to the dying of your loved one on your journey together through Alzheimer's disease.

Part Two

Practical Help and Resources

Shadows X

Chapter Fourteen

At Home with Alzheimer's Disease

In March of 2012 I attended a presentation by Dr. Paul Raia, Clinical Adviser to the Alzheimer's Association of Massachusetts and New Hampshire, at Whitney Place Assisted Living Facility in Natick, Massachusetts. I connected powerfully to what he had to say, as so much of what he described I had already been through, or discovered on my own, in my journey with Mom. He provided form, structure and a name for many elements of living at home during this journey with Alzheimer's; in essence, he connected the dots for me. As I said in the beginning chapter of this book, when you stand back from a thing in time or space it takes on shape, meaning and form. Dr. Raia allowed me to stand back and see the experiences I had lived through with Mom from a structured, empowered perspective. I have recorded here for you the facts and information he presented about his Habilitation Therapy program for living at home successfully with your loved one. I include my own comments and insights for you as well.

According to Dr. Raia, there are many current and stunning facts connected with Alzheimer's disease in the U.S. At the present time *over 5.4 million people* have Alzheimer's disease (AD)—a number that is expected to triple over the next twenty years as the baby-boomer generation ages. Alzheimer's health care costs currently run about *$236 billion annually*—also on the rise. AD is the sixth leading cause of death for adults, and is the *only* major cause that shows an increase in the death rate each year.

However, the most interesting figures are about home caregivers. There are *15.9 million* caregivers at home, providing over *18 billion hours* worth of unpaid care to their loved ones each year. This is a staggering amount of care, and it is crucial to the nation's health care system. This means that you, as caregiver, are by no means an isolated individual at home struggling your way through an unexpected life challenge. You are part of a growing, critically important community, and there are many resources available to support and inform you in your journey with your loved one. As medical research races against time to find treatments and cures for this unrelenting disease, you hold the front-line positions in Alzheimer's care by keeping your loved ones at home, comfortable, safe, and feeling as secure as possible each and every day for as long as possible.

Since caregivers themselves are in an at-risk category, Dr. Raia took time to go over risk factors for this capricious disease. While actual triggers and courses can be as individual as each person that Alzheimer's affects, there are identified factors that come into play in the development of AD. No one factor in particular has been identified as causing Alzheimer's. Neither how these factors combine nor the number of factors necessary to bring about the onset of the disease is, as yet, clearly understood.*

Risk Factors for Developing Later Onset Alzheimer's Disease:

1. Age

15% of people aged 65–74,
44% of people aged 75–84, and
37% of people over age 85 develop Alzheimer's.

Currently, the over-80 population is the fastest-growing segment of America's population.

2. Genes

At present, genetic inheritance plays an unclear role in the development of Alzheimer's disease. Having one close relative with the disease presents a 12% probability of developing Alzheimer's; two close relatives with the disease increases that likelihood to 25%.

3. Cardiovascular Health

Poor cardiovascular health is a contributing factor.

* *Early onset Alzheimer's disease or "familial Alzheimer's disease" occurs before age 65, and has been determined to be the result of several rare genes, according to the Alzheimer's Association. See* www.alz.org/alzheimers_disease_early_onset.asp

4. Diabetes

Dr. Raia explained that there are some studies describing Alzheimer's disease as a unique form of diabetes of the brain. We still have much to learn, but apparently diabetes itself is a factor.

5. Chronic Depression

While Dr. Raia did not elaborate on this factor, I feel that constant negative thoughts deplete energy, form negative patterns in the brain and our behavior, and thereby possibly contribute to the onset of Alzheimer's. Perhaps some of the depression that professionals attribute to this disease could be the less inhibited expression of a preceding, untreated, state of depression. Mom was not a happy woman, and I have heard of other instances of dispirited loved ones developing Alzheimer's. How we greet our older age and its challenges matters. I would love to see more research and information on this subject.

6. Head Injury

Head injuries create a risk at any time in life, not just in the later years, and are definitely a risk for Alzheimer's.

7. Stress

Being a caregiver is a risk factor for the disease itself, due to the stress it can cause. When your body produces cortisol, a common by-product of stress, it combines with cholesterol in your system. This results in a decrease in your body's ability to dissolve the beta-amyloid proteins responsible for Alzheimer's. While many people produce beta-amyloid proteins, not all develop AD. Stress weakens your body's protection against factors contributing to Alzheimer's.

While risk factors 1 and 2 are beyond our ability to change, every other risk factor can be impacted by making healthful decisions and by developing healthy practices in life. Many people know enough to invest in and plan for a healthy financial retirement. Plan for a *physically* healthy retirement as well. Healthy aging will reduce your retirement costs and increase your quality of life. You *can* make a difference in your risk factors!

In the meantime, if you are a caregiver, make yourself knowledgeable about Alzheimer's disease. Your local Alzheimer's Association chapter can provide you with contacts for information, programs, and resources to help you. Running headlong into unforeseen problems and bewildering behaviors when information is available to equip you to cope with these challenges creates unnecessary stress—not only for yourself, but also for your loved one. Being prepared with this knowledge and these resources can do much to reduce the stress that Alzheimer's brings into your life.

Caregiver's Lament

Oh, where has my loved one gone?
Oh, there am I gone to as well.
Our lives are turned off
Upside down, inside out.
This was not the path I had planned.
This was not the design of my heart.
Oh, help me, help me, to do my part.

What, Exactly, Is Alzheimer's Disease?

According to Dr Raia, Alzheimer's disease is a progressive, debilitating brain disease resulting in death. Up to two-thirds of the brain is physically gone by the time of death. Mom had frontal temporal dementia as well as AD (not an uncommon combination) and her last CAT scan showed large empty spaces, called "potholes" in her frontal areas, along with very little remaining brain mass in the hippocampus. She was in a skilled nursing facility, wheelchair bound, and unable to perform any activities of daily living on her own.

As a caretaker for someone with Alzheimer's, you are tending to the complete and final loss of the ability of a human brain to carry out its functions. You are there to guide, protect, care for, plan, support, and bury your loved one. Creating a good environment for your loved one to live these final years peacefully and securely—whether at home or in a care facility—and then providing the opportunity for your loved one to die with dignity is the final part of your journey together on earth.

Welcome to the greatest challenge of human life—that of helping another face his or her end with courage, peacefulness and dignity.

Alzheimer's disease, as Dr. Raia points out, starts in the *temporal areas* of the brain—the ones responsible for short-term memory and decision-making. We make decisions every day. We take two or three options, compare and contrast them, and choose a course of action. In early-stage Alzheimer's, the ability to compare and contrast ideas goes away. This part of the brain shuts down first. Thus unusual behaviors appear first. People with AD may do out-of-character things or say things you would not normally expect of them. It is so easy to attribute these behaviors to some other cause and to overlook these early signs. Early detection can result in the prescription of medications that may slow the symptoms of memory loss and give you some much-appreciated, precious time with your loved one. Use this time to talk and plan and face life together while your loved one is still able to join with you in making plans. Soon enough you will be alone on your care-taking journey, unable to decipher what their true wishes may have been.

During one of our conversations, Mom was actually relieved when I told her she had Alzheimer's disease. I am sure she went through much inner turmoil over what was happening to her. It was a welcome relief to her on many levels to have another person fully accept that she had AD without diminishing a respectful opinion of her. At the time, I thought this relief short-lived. When I told her "the truth," she was already so deeply affected by Alzheimer's that she could not remember what I had said for more than a very few minutes at a time. However, the emotional relief it gave her lasted beyond her memory of what I said—relief she deserved. It was a great comfort to me to learn that stepping out of the family bondage of denial to tell her the loving truth she was searching for was of positive emotional benefit to her—that it brought her a solace and peacefulness longer-lasting than her dry-erase memory of the words themselves.

As the disease progresses it deeply affects the *hippocampus,* the area in the lower back of the brain responsible for categorization and storage of information. Not only can your loved one not compare information, he or she cannot store it. Dr Raia describes the hippocampus as our internal filing system: a piece of information comes in, is put in a folder, labeled, and put in the appropriate file. Most memory issues with normal aging have to do with finding that file again to access the information. Sometimes it may take a day or two for that name to pop back into the current file, but it does. In Alzheimer's, the information comes in, but there is no categorization process—no folder with a label that can be put into a file for later retrieval. The information is never stored. Dr. Raia calls this a "broken hippocampus." He says it is very important to understand this basic element of the disease, which is responsible for the questions and strange journeys you will take with your loved one. There is no way for him or her to recall what you just said. Each time is essentially the first time your loved one has heard your information.

Other Effects of Alzheimer's

When someone has Alzheimer's disease, their eyes and ears continue to function, but the brain can no longer properly process the information coming from them. Thus, sight is affected as well as the ability to understand language. I like to think of the human brain as being our receiving, processing and transmitting device—in addition to being our data storage center. Much like a radio, the brain receives signals and transmits them. The good news is that even when a radio is not functioning properly, the signal is still there. To me, this means that the life and energy of your loved one abides in them, but their usual ability to store, process and transmit information is not working well. You will, however, find your loved one's spirit unimpaired! Below are some other ways the brain's receiver-transmitter stops processing.

Vision

In early- to mid-stage AD, depth and peripheral vision are extremely impaired, along with spatial memory, which means knowing where you are in relation to everything around you, and where you are going. Early on, your loved one sees only the middle range of vision, as if looking through a cardboard tube that blocks out everything else. Peripheral vision is gone, as is the person's ability to orient themself to where he or she is. Therefore, no matter how competent they may seem either to themselves or possibly even to you, driving is hazardous for your loved one to do. I remember when Mom's doctor suggested she not drive anymore, we thought there was something wrong with the doctor! Read on for techniques and helps on how to approach—or rather distract—your loved one from this and other activities that may no longer be safe for them to do "as usual."

By mid-stage Alzheimer's, the ability to perceive shades of color disappears. Your loved one will be able to see primary colors—much like a baby whose vision has not yet developed. Bright red will attract their attention. For instance, wearing bright red lipstick may help when communicating with your loved one. He or she will more easily see your lips form the words. My brightly colored nail polish pulled Mom's eyes to every movement of my hands.

Personality and Motor Skills

Mid-stage Alzheimer's also affects the *frontal temporal area* of the brain. This is where the sense of personality resides: the ability to understand ourselves and use insight, and the ability to control our behavior. Hallucinations can result. These are not the big, wild hallucinations you see in the movies; they are everyday things that make it seem as if your loved one has momentarily departed from reality. Their reality shifts as their ability to interpret what they see and hear changes. It was so natural for me to walk into Mom's care facility and stop to listen to people's stories—how they think they are at work and don't like their job anymore, for example. These departures from what is "real" often upset family members, causing them to try to pull their loved ones back into reality by opposing their story with "the truth." What the person in the scene above is *really* communicating is their unhappiness with where they are. So I listen, give appropriate assent to their concerns, and tell them, for example, that their lunch break is coming soon; perhaps they can have a good lunch, then take care of the problem. They are comforted by the fact that I stopped and listened. I have seen an agitated resident become a peaceful person simply because someone entered *their* reality.

There is a small area in the front of the brain, the *ventromedial area,* that controls how we interact with people—our morality center, as it were. Alzheimer's affects this area also, resulting in some strange interactions with others—behaviors that can be out-of-the-ordinary for your loved one, including flirtation! Mom was a femme fatale for a while.

Motor skills, from fine to gross, are eventually affected as the disease moves to the *cerebellum* and eventually to the *brain stem,* which controls the automatic functions of our bodies. The body cannot maintain itself. Reflexes go, and the ability to swallow is eventually lost. The brain slowly shuts down the body as its ability to perform life-giving activities degenerates.

Language

In later stages of Alzheimer's, language is impaired—both the ability to understand it and to produce it. Near the end Mom babbled a delightful stream of completely incomprehensible commentary, with a few emphatic words or phrases peppered in: "Yes," or "That's good," or "I hope so," yet her eyes were focused on my face, and her every expression told me of her care and concern about everything–what was happening to her, how I am, how the children are. It was all there in the wrinkle of her brow, the tone of her voice, the look in her eyes.

So how do we live with this very terrible, irreversible progression, when sight and hearing, communication, orientation, memory and personal expression are beyond connection? How do we relate to our loved one now?

Habilitation Therapy

Help is available through the practice of *Habilitation Therapy*. According to Dr. Raia, the lower central part of the brain, known as the *amygdala*, remains intact to the very end of this disease. The amygdala is the center responsible for emotions. It is the part of the brain that is present and able to respond. Dr. Raia has developed a method of responding to and working with the amygdala called Habilitation Therapy, which you can use at home to help create a more peaceful and happy experience of daily living for yourself and your loved one.

Perhaps your loved one was never very comfortable expressing emotions. Perhaps you are not, either. Perhaps you consider the whole idea of talking about feelings to be too emotional. For now, please relax, take a deep breath, clear your mind, and read on.

One might have said my mother was a bit proper and not given to showing emotions in public. One could also possibly have said that she was angry and bitter about some things in her life, or sometimes a bit sharp-tongued or difficult. Interestingly enough, one of the first things my sister and I noticed about Mom in her disease was that, as she lost some negative memories, she detached from the negative emotions associated with them. She became quite open, funny and much more gentle. There is a way in which the disease wipes the slate clean, and while we mourn the loss of memories and capacities we loved, there is no doubt that old hurts and emotional patterns associated with them disappear as well. In essence, you as caregiver are given an ever-cleaner slate upon which to write. The story of the path you and your loved one take together is very much in your hands. Habilitation Therapy will enable you to write a script with which you can both be more at peace in your daily journey.

First let me clarify, per Dr. Raia, that Habilitation Therapy is *not* restorative: it will not bring back any capacities your loved one has lost. What it *does* is maximize your loved one's potential by working with positive emotions. The goal of Habilitation Therapy is to produce a positive response through positive emotional connection. As you work with the concepts of Habilitation Therapy for your loved one, you will find yourself redirecting your own energies in positive ways as well. This becomes a two-way benefit for both of you.

Reading through the information that follows will help you get an idea of how to bring new behaviors and responses into in your life at home with your loved one. For further information or clarification, or to receive more specific help, please contact your local Alzheimer's chapter.

Domains

The first concept in Habilitation Therapy is the concept of *domains.* Domains are areas where you as caregiver can influence brain behavior, or response from your loved one. It is vitally important for those of us on this path to understand that *no behavior is random.* All behavior is a form of communication. If you look at the world and those you love with these new eyes of understanding, you open yourself up to communicating on much deeper levels. Once your loved one's verbal communication is diminished, non-verbal communication becomes your source of connection to them. Behavior *is* non-verbal communication.

Triggers

Behavior is triggered in two different ways. As your loved one progresses in the disease and is not able to tell you when something hurts or is uncomfortable, his or her behavior will let you know. *Internal triggers* for problem behaviors may be such things as pain from any source, including teeth or dentures, constipation, dehydration and depression. Internal triggers are hard to discern and are usually responsible for sudden behavioral changes. It is generally accepted that things such as urinary tract infections can cause sudden unhappy and unacceptable behaviors.

Mom was unhappy being in a nursing facility that did not meet her needs and was full of new situations and routines that frightened her. When this was exacerbated by an undetected urinary tract infection, she became combative, and her facility's doctor wrote an order for "observation." Mom ended up in the hospital emergency room, followed by a ten-day stay in a geriatric psychiatric unit, as I described in an earlier chapter. Here they treated the infection, but also prescribed psychotropic, behavior-modifying drugs to control her "unwanted" behavior. We moved her from that facility into one we thought would be a better fit for her.

Mom again became combative while in this new rehabilitative facility, and was sent back to the geriatric psychiatric unit where her medication levels were "adjusted." During this period of what became over-medication, I actually thought Mom was going to die soon. She was extremely lethargic and unresponsive, and lost the ability to do many things she had done for herself before these drugs were prescribed. The second time this facility complained of her combativeness and sent her back to the geriatric psychiatric unit, my sister and I moved Mom back to her first facility, in a different unit, where she received care that made her feel happy and secure.

Some of Mom's distresses were *externally triggered* events: those happening outside herself. In the second facility, the staff were not properly trained to care for dementia patients, which caused Mom much distress. An external trigger usually develops over time instead of suddenly, and is sometimes hard to see because it happens so gradually. An external trigger is, however, one that can be identified and changed. Just ask: "What is the behavior that is happening? Where is the behavior taking place? When does it happen? Who is present?" Listen to your answers to these questions. We were constantly being told that Mom was combative. The reality was that Mom was unhappy with and constantly frightened by the abrupt treatment of her caregivers. Her *behavior* was her communication. *We* were the ones who had trouble listening.

It is my hope that by reading this book you will become more aware when such instances occur, and that you will look and listen to what your loved one is telling you with their behavior, recognizing it as an instance of non-verbal communication. He or she is *not* impaired in their ability to know and communicate what is good for them and what is not.

How does recognizing and working with these two types of triggers help you at home with your loved one? Dr. Raia has identified "Domains of Habilitation" as different areas of daily living which can be enhanced by the use of habilitation therapy. By identifying them in your particular home environment, you, as caregiver, can influence the behavior of your loved one to your mutual benefit and peacefulness. So much of Alzheimer's disease seems to put one out of control–you never know what is going to happen next. It is good to realize that there are areas where you *do* have control, and that you can use them to make a positive difference in both your lives.

Domains of Habilitation:

1. Physical Environment
2. Communication
3. Personal Care
4. Structure of the Day

1. Physical Environment

Dr Raia's advice is to create a supportive environment. Design a home environment that enables your loved one to function better. Because of vision impairment, people with AD need more light —but not glaring light; they need consistent, high levels of light. Enhance their function with color: use bold primary colors to identify functional areas of the home that are important for your loved one, like the bathroom. Your local Alzheimer's chapter has consultants who can meet with you in your home to help you create an environment that enhances and enables your loved one to live a more normal life. If your loved one had a broken leg, for example, you would immediately make the changes necessary to help them get around and be safe at home. Creating a safe, clear, function-enhancing environment for your loved one who suffers from AD is no different.

2. Communication

When confronted by difficult behavior, ask, "Is this behavior caused by something I did or did not say?" Communicating with someone with Alzheimer's is a new way of using language. You may need to consciously alter some of the language patterns you have developed in your relationship over the years, to allow for your loved one's continually changing level of comprehension.

When communicating with your loved one, always approach them from the front. Do *not* talk from behind them, which is outside of their range of perception. Say his or her name and your name *every time.* Move to your loved one's level: if sitting, sit. Move to his or her *left* side–after you have established eye contact from the front. This causes your loved one to move their head to the left, which activates the right side of the brain–the emotion center.

Chunk the information you give them. Chunking is breaking down a task or activity into simple, directional steps. For example, asking your loved one to help you set the table actually involves many complex operations he or she may no longer be able to string together. So a seemingly simple task may present a huge challenge for them, which produces a negative emotional reaction. Instead, say, "Come with me," and walk over to the cupboard. Then say, "Open the cabinet," and "Take out the dish," and so on. There are many steps involved in what we think of as simple, everyday activities. It is almost as if you are programming a computer to perform a function. Each step must be defined. The only difference here is, of course, that your loved one has no storage capability and will not be able to recall the programming. He or she will have to be directed *each and every time.* This is a brave new way of life for you as caregiver.

The goal of Habilitation Therapy is to bring about positive emotions. The only way to change your loved one's behavior is by what you do and say, and by the environment you create for them. Take responsibility for making the changes needed to do this. One way is to avoid using the word "no" with your loved one. Saying no implies confrontation and creates a negative emotional response. Use *time* (It is your friend!) to change your loved one's original intention and refocus their attention (thought). Redirect action (behavior) by using food. Food is very important at this stage of the disease. If your loved one wants to drive their car, you can say for example, "That's a great idea! Hey, let's have a sandwich first." Affirm your loved one and his or her intentions, then *redirect the action.* This is what I did with some of the residents in Mom's facility, and it works.

It is also very important to listen for what your loved one is *really* expressing when he or she talks about some situation that you know is not real. Perhaps your loved one is certain they have seen a family member who died years ago. Ask yourself, "What does the relationship with that family member mean to my loved one? What is he or she looking for: love, acceptance, feeling safe?" Enter into your loved one's reality. Ask him or her to tell you about their relationship to the family member. *Give no correction, no reminding of reality.* Imagine the sadness you bring about when you dutifully remind them that this person is dead. A minute later they will not remember what you said. But, since the emotional center is not impaired, he or she will remain sad and not know why. For example, Mom's *feeling* of relief when I revealed the cause of her confusion as Alzheimer's disease was longer-lived than her *memory* of my telling her. She "remembered" her feeling of peacefulness.

Look beneath the words—don't just respond to what you hear. "I want to go home" may mean that your loved one does not *feel* at home. Create a sense of purpose, meaning, and belonging around them where they are. A more meaningful interpretation of "You took my pocketbook" may be to hear "I am missing my identity." Look at to how to create a sense of identity for your loved one, and redirect them to a positive activity. We used to give Mom another pocketbook with much fanfare: "How beautifully this goes with your outfit! You look lovely! Let's go out to dinner!" The goal here is to create a positive emotional response. Mom would remember the satisfied feeling of being well put-together long after she had forgotten about her pocketbook! (We had a good supply!)

Personal Care

Personal care comes about because someone gives consent. Giving consent comes from relationship. Your loved one has Alzheimer's disease. You have to re-establish relationship each time you approach. Establish relationship to gain consent.

Some tips on how this works:

Make a direct connection with your loved one. Clearly identify who you are and what your relationship is. I always said, "Hi Mom, it's Deb" whenever I approached my mother. It is very important to re-establish relationship *each time* you approach your loved one, once they have reached a point where they clearly seem not to remember you. If you turn away to water a plant and come back into their range of vision, you need to re-establish contact so they can participate in what you are doing with them. Sit and chat with your loved one for a minute. Establish a positive emotional relationship, then start personal care. I always told Mom what I was doing, because many normal activities were no longer familiar rhythms in her life. Even when putting hand cream on her hands or lip balm on her lips she would startle if I did not explain and gain her consent first. It was most important that she knew who I was and that I was doing something good and caring for her. I talked to Mom while I did any personal care task. It helped to reassure her, and calmed her to hear my voice. If something had disturbed her, I responded by acknowledging her discomfort then moved to make her feel comfortable and secure again.

However, do not do something for someone that he or she can still do. You will speed up the loss of their ability to do those things. Let them do whatever they can for themselves. This is love. Just like a child who will never learn to ride a bike until you let go, don't jump into a situation where your loved one is struggling. Let them do a little wrestling with the task. Take a deep breath to slow yourself down.

Creating a positive emotional response reinforces your loved one's sense of security and belonging. It helps to prevent the build-up of a negative emotional state and can reduce the "sundowning" effect (anxiety, agitation and disorientation) experienced by dementia patients later in the afternoon. Another cause of sundowning, according to Dr. Raia, is sleep deprivation. Your loved one needs at least four consecutive hours of sleep at night. Dr. Raia suggested that it can be helpful to deny short naps later in the day, keep him or her awake, and add vitamin D at night to help them get a good night's sleep. You will enjoy that, too. Mom's husband still could not sleep more than a very few hours at night after the past several years of caregiving—even though Mom had been in a nursing home for two years. By adding some vitamins D and B, he started to get some of his equilibrium back. It is slow going to regain the restful ground lost during the home-caregiving part of this illness. The older you are, the greater the toll it takes upon your rest. Ensuring a good night's sleep will benefit both of you immensely.

Structure of the Day

Finally, create structure in your loved one's day. More structure leads to a more peaceful environment by reducing negative, damaging behaviors that can occur when nothing is in place to direct your loved one's energy and attention. Try to set up a daily routine of meaningful engagement. Include things your loved one likes to do. Many communities have special programs and events for persons with AD and their caregivers. Take advantage of the resources of your community and your local Alzheimer's chapter to fill your life with meaningful activities and supportive people around both of you. It is most important not to retreat from life and the company of others as you walk this path. Although Mom did not want to go to her church (where she was afraid people she knew would see and know she was not her normal self) there were many activities and centers around them which could have provided Mom and Tom with a greater sense of connection and care if they had chosen to participate. Whether you find activities outside your home or simply develop delightful routines to engage your loved one at home, which Tom did so successfully for Mom, create a warm, structured, environmentally friendly place where positive emotional responses are enabled and enhanced. You will both live more peacefully and comfortably through this time together.

It is my observation that many of the behaviors and diminished functions exhibited in everyday life by someone with Alzheimer's are similar to the process of the growth of children–in reverse. Children's brains grow and develop during childhood, while our loved ones' brains correspondingly lose their capacities during Alzheimer's. If you draw upon the same attitude and patience used in parenting–that of loving and encouraging your loved one while being willing and able to accept them where they are in their developmental phase–it makes the journey a little easier to handle emotionally. Much of the horror we experience as caregivers is a reaction to the loss of mental maturity in one we have related to as an adult for many years. If we can shift our thinking and frame of reference to accepting the increasingly simplified, child-like functioning of our loved one, this frame of reference can do much to increase patience and love and reduce the stress and pain in caregiving. While those with Alzheimer's disease are by no means children, the patience and acceptance you used during parenting will help create a positive emotional atmosphere that will bring more peacefulness to you and your loved one on this journey.

Memories

The frosts of cold November
Chill into bone and heart.
Soft summer remembers,
Drifting, as we part,
In its embers . . .

Cold fears and flames impart
A crystal-cleanness as we start
To fall in love with memories.
Clear, dewing drops
Distilled within our hearts
To Keep
Sleep,
Weep,
Softly,
Gently,
Deeply.

Tree

Chapter Fifteen

Alzheimer's and Caregivers Resources

Caring for your loved one at home is a monumental task! The Alzheimer's Association has numerous resources to assist you in finding services and agencies that can help with added care in your home, and with full-time residential and nursing care when and if you should need it. Here are charts of the various types of resources available to support you as a caregiver. They are taken in part from the Alzheimer's Association brochure, "Choosing a Residential Care Facility," with added comments based on my family's experience. When we started our searches we had no clear knowledge of any of the specific services, functions or limitations of these resources; they were unknown entities, and this helpful brochure was not available. **I am not a professional reference for these services, or for placing your loved one in any facility**. I am simply sharing the Alzheimer's Association's information and our observations gained during our search, hoping to help you realize the great difference in the types of care available and the services offered.

There are many differences in the services and the funding of these entities, in and of themselves, and as governed by local states. Our experiences were based in the state of Massachusetts. Some suggestions:

- Check your own state for resources and regulations regarding each type of facility listed.
- Be aware that within state regulations there are further differences in individual facilities and in the breadth of services offered.

The Alzheimer's Association has a good website at *www.communityresourcefinder.org* which allows you to create a customized search of resources in your local area. If you are a long-distance caregiver, it is invaluable to be able to search in your loved one's local community from your distant location. It is important to maximize your precious time at your loved one's location by doing this kind of research in advance!

Residential Care

Type of Facility	Description	Services	Comments
Independent Living Facilities	These are age-segregated facilities where healthy, mobile seniors live on their own with a minimum of assistance.	These facilities generally provide meals (for an extra cost), wheels (ditto), check-in (included) and EMT service when needed (also extra). Some facilities are complexes which include a Memory Unit for mid-stage Alzheimer's and dementia residents.	We never used one of these for Mom. Tom was Mom's independent living provider!
Adult Family Homes (Can be covered by Medicaid)	An AFH is a residential home, licensed to care for up to six adults not related by blood or marriage to the person or persons providing the services.	An AFH provides room and meals, laundry, supervision, assistance with activities of daily living and personal care. Some homes provide nursing or other special care. *(Be sure to ask!)*	We never used this type of program for Mom.
Assisted Living Communities with Memory Care Units (Private pay)	Assisted living communities are designed to provide residents with assistance with basic activities of daily living such as bathing, grooming, dressing and other activities.	Some states also allow assisted living communities to offer medication assistance and/or reminders. They do not offer complex medical services, and some offer a higher level of service for a higher price.	Be sure to ask what your chosen facility specifically does and does not do! We tried moving Mom to one of these and it was not a good choice. She had much less capacity than the other residents and soon needed more medical care than this facility could provide.
Residential Facilities (Can be covered by Medicaid)	These facilities provide custodial care to persons who, because of physical, mental or emotional disorders, are not able to live independently.	Medical and custodial oversight is provided, usually with state funding.	Custodial care is *not* dementia care! Be sure to ask, as some facilities do offer dementia care.
Skilled Nursing Facilities (Nursing Homes) (Can be covered by Medicaid)	This is a health-care institution that meets federal criteria for Medicaid and Medicare reimbursement for nursing care.	These facilities provide supervision of the care of every patient by a physician, at least one full-time registered nurse on staff, the maintenance of records concerning the care and condition of every patient, nursing care 24 hours a day, facilities for storing and dispensing drugs, and implementation of a utilization review plan.	This is where Mom was. By end-stage of this disease, your loved one may need all the benefits of a skilled nursing facility. Some "complex" type facilities offer escalating services at different units in their complexes, allowing for progressive care.

Medical Care

Type of Facility	Description	Services	Comments
Hospice	Hospice is a service for the care of the dying or incurably ill. It offers a type of care and a philosophy of care that focuses on the easing of a terminally ill or seriously ill patient's pain and symptoms. Hospice is available in a number of care settings from home to skilled nursing and everything in between.	Hospice care focuses on bringing comfort, self-respect, and tranquility to people in the final stages of life. Patients' symptoms and pain are controlled, goals of care are discussed, and emotional needs are supported. Hospice believes that the end of life is not a medical experience; it is a human experience that benefits from the expert medical and holistic support that hospice offers.	My note: as such, hospice covers end-of-life care for Alzheimer's patients who are seriously impaired in their abilities to take care of their daily needs. The old adage of "six months to live" does not apply to Alzheimer's patients. Hospice was a wonderful resource for us with Mom for many months. It is necessary for hospice facilities to re-certify every 30-60 days to maintain Medicaid funding. Your loved one may not always re-qualify.
Hospitals	A hospital is an institution providing medical and surgical treatment and nursing care for sick or injured people.	I am not even going to attempt to describe services, except to say that there are many types and sizes and specialties associated with various hospital facilities. It is always good to know your local hospitals, their offerings, programs, and areas of expertise, and the reputation of their doctors and staff. By the time we need their services we are too immediately in need of them to research their effectiveness.	Beware of Geriatric Psychiatric Units that deal with behavior from a medication standpoint—Mom's prescribed medication was more than necessary for an overly long period because of her stay in these units. Question medications and don't hesitate to request lowering or removing them! Beware of hospitals in general—they do not understand the needs of dementia patients well. Mom's bedsores were directly caused by insufficient turning during her hospital stay for a urinary tract infection!

There are many differences among types of care facilities. It is most important to assess as well as you can where your loved one is in their journey and where their next steps may take them. The goal is to choose a facility that will provide adequately for the level of care they now need and the level of care they are likely to need going forward. It is also essential to have a staff that is familiar with and trained in dementia and Alzheimer's care, *with an active dementia program for residents*. Just because a facility cares for residents with mental impairment does not mean it has any specifically developed Alzheimer's program or staff training!

Some additional tips I would suggest when you are ready to begin your search:

- Know the elements that contribute to a successful environment for those with Alzheimer's. For instance, the use of color and habilitative (positive) response therapy, "camouflaged" exits, visually esthetic interest points for residents, aromatherapy, a calming environment, and the use of memory stimulation through association are all things to look for in a facility. See Chapters 14 and 17 for more details.
- Develop a set of criteria that you can use across the board for each facility. See the Alzheimer's Association's brochure on "Choosing a Residential Care Facility" for a take-along survey of facilities.
- Visit your top choices more than once. First impressions can change upon revisiting. Daily atmospheres change within the facility. Staff is different on different shifts. Know your facility.
- Ask questions. When you are shopping for services for your loved one, there are no wrong questions.
- Get some help. Searching for and selecting a facility is emotionally,mentally and physically exhausting.
- Understand that once your loved one is placed, you will continue to be an essential part of their proper care.

Community and State Services

Check with each resource directly for an expanded listing of specific services they provide:

- Aging and disability resource centers
- Adult day programs
- Area agencies on aging
- Geriatric care managers
- Home care
- Home health care

- Relocation managers
- State units on aging
- Title VI agencies
- Transportation services

For "area agencies" please contact your local senior citizens' center, community center, or health center for your specific community-related resources. These agencies can be a vibrant, caring connection for you as you begin your search for support, and as you work to create a positive structure for your new life with Alzheimer's.

Searching the Internet by any of these categories will yield many individual agencies and service providers to assist you. Relocation managers are becoming a very important resource as distant caregivers decide to move their loved ones closer to be with them. Moves across state lines can be tricky and involve legal issues of guardianship, etc. The Alzheimer's Association is working to reduce these issues for caregivers. You may call their 24-hour help line at 800-272-3900 for assistance in all of these heart-rending care decisions. Help is available in 140 different languages at any time of the day or night.

Additionally, check out the resources of your local Alzheimer's Association chapter **online** at *www.alz.org*. The website offers:

- Educational programs
- Support groups
- Early-stage programs
- Events

All of these will help you by providing information and support, assessment tools, inspirational stories and opportunities to get you both out of the house and be engaged with others.

Shadows XI

Chapter Sixteen

Roses and Reiki

Roses and Reiki

for Mom,
who can take
all we can give
today

Reiki and Roses
for moments'
sweet posies
that chime eternity
today

A time of quiet
some caring and sharing
A gift to give and stay
Roses and Reiki
today

The final gift this journey with my mother imparted to me was to learn Reiki, a spiritual healing practice that deeply relaxes, refreshes and renews by supporting inner balance and wholeness, usually through gentle touch. It was discovered and developed in Japan in the early 1900s by Dr.

Mikao Usui. Using Reiki with Mom brought about a beautiful connection between us, as well as increased peacefulness and well-being for us both. I have provided Reiki to others on their journey through Alzheimer's since this time, and I have discovered it to be an invaluable tool for those with dementia and for their caregivers.[†]

Shortly after Mom began receiving Reiki from me and members of our hospice team, she came successfully off of a permanent catheter after two years of treatment following renal failure. We were also able to take her completely off the psychotropic drugs. Reiki is used today in many medical settings.[‡]

Even though the psychotropic drug doses were small, there was a huge difference in Mom's alertness and responsiveness once they were stopped. She became a lot more fun and expressed more of her own personality. Listen to and deal with your loved one's acting-out behaviors in positive ways, and keep psychotropic drugs out of the picture as much as possible! I cannot stress this enough; and Reiki can help.

Make wise decisions about which facility you will choose for your loved one. Always look for an established dementia care facility with well-cared-for, peaceful, alert residents. Make absolutely certain that the staff will inform you of any medication changes.

Mom did very well in her nursing home. My church was my Sunday morning visits to see her. She was always happy to see me and our visits were filled with precious moments of love and connection and Reiki. Every week I brought her fresh flowers and we cut and arranged them together—she with the loosened bunch on her lap, me taking each one in its turn to hold up to her gaze, for her to smell, and to remember her joy of gardening.

---

† See APA article: Bier, D. 2012. *Reiki's Use in Dementia Patients and for Their Caregivers.* Psych Central.

‡ We do not yet have adequate research models for tracking practices which promote wellness; research models are geared to only evaluate drug treatments for specific illnesses. See http://www.centerforreikiresearch.org/ RRdownloads/RRSample.pdf for more information.

She babbled delightedly at me. We had whole conversations–me interpreting her stream of commentary, her looks and eye expressions, filling in the substance with the questions I knew she was asking: "How far did you travel? What direction did you come from? How is the family? What am I doing here?" I could tell how she was by one look at her face; recognizable words were not necessary for our conversation.

I used her favorite Oil of Olay face cream and gently moisturized her face. I very gently massaged her hands with organic lavender cream. We ventured out to the garden when the weather permitted, to view the flowers and vegetables growing, or visited the sunroom in the colder weather, which usually brought on a contented little nap. I gave her Reiki to soothe and heal any of her wants and needs.

Most often, I would stay and feed her a pureed feast of a Sunday dinner–one spoonful at a time, with thickened liquids to assuage her thirst. Sometimes, she was just asleep, and I sang her lullabies and read poetry out loud, or sat and wrote or drew.

This was the peaceful, secure, well-cared-for time we shared, waiting for The Next. Little weekly depletions happened very slowly. I became ready. She became ready. And we all went to the end together. I cried. If she could have, she would still have comforted me.

Because of the work I did to cope with my own reactions and fears, and because I came into a new place of understanding about life and death and Alzheimer's Disease through my personal daily Reiki practice, I created a new relationship with Mom, honoring and supporting her in her journey. This was a shift of which I was not fully aware. She sensed and responded to that in me, which created that new space we inhabited together.

It is my sincere hope that by having read this book you will be empowered to create a new relationship with *your* loved one by releasing the guilt and grief, anger, fear and pain that are Alzheimer's main accompaniments. By doing so, you may come into a new place of understanding that will allow for greater joy, awareness and celebration of your loved one's indomitable spirit of life.

Finally, if you have it in you, write out your journey from the depths of your heart. Write your memories. Share them with your loved one. Tell your loved one how much you love him or her. View the beautiful places of your lives together and know that you have both enjoyed the gift of a wondrous life with each other.

Queen

Like a queen, she sits in her Chair
gently hoisted from here to there
while we minister to her with care.

She is serenely unaware
nodding and smiling as we wheel her
slowly past her fans.
Occasionally she bestows
a regal hello.

But more often than not
has no conception
of our work to feed and care-take.
She has more important things to do
than notice our labors.

She has to follow through,
complete her Course,
her inner journey
to places we cannot go
where only the demented know
the secrets they hold within.

Beyond the scope of our ken
they live their lives over again
working the re-write
of their souls
into knowing, being, whole. . . .

The Way Home

Chapter Seventeen

Namaste: End-of-Life Caring and Honoring

How hard it is to think the thoughts,
say the words,
hold the cup
of parting in our hands;
drink from either side
and share with friends
the banns of leaving, and our ends.

Many cultures have developed time-honored traditions of leaving and dying. In our mixed modern culture, we have disconnected from these roots and traditions, and so have lost our ability to be present to the end of life in a meaningful way. We house the sick away from us in institutions. We get sickness and death over with as quickly as possible so we can to go back to our daily duties and routines. As we have seen so far in our journey together, Alzheimer's will not allow us the luxury of that denial. With this disease we live with death and dying, and have a unique opportunity to connect with our loved ones in new ways–to be with and honor them in their final steps here. *Namaste Care* can facilitate that connection.

Namaste Care is based on the "Tree of Life" or the *Kabbalah*, and is the concept of *namaste*, which has become my mantra and greeting, and means "to honor the spirit within." I was introduced to the concept through the book, *The End-of-Life Namaste Care Program for People with Dementia*, by Joyce Simard. The book was given to me as a gift by someone who was working in the health care industry. I am passing its wisdom on to you. Having incorporated many of the concepts from the book during my visits with my mother, I can say the results were wonderful. Unlike others of my family who were at a loss over how to be with Mom, I looked forward to my visits with her.

Namaste Care is devoted to building a listening, caring relationship with advanced dementia patients in which they are empowered by recognition of themselves by others as fully alive, honored beings. Namaste Care is the way to learn new connections and a way to explore and learn the different ways and levels we have to stay connected, express love, and allow our loved ones to make their own journeys.

It will most likely be time to start your nursing home or constant in-home skilled care search somewhere around mid- to late-mid-stage Alzheimer's. Please start it early enough so that you will have time to get used to the strangeness of this new world of care, early enough so that you will be able to develop the ability to see the difference between well-cared-for and neglected or drugged residents. The thought of this process is often so abhorrent that families put this off until it becomes a necessity. By then, you will not have the time to adjust and will not be able to judge what you are looking at.

I suggest that you look for a facility with a Namaste Care program. As Joyce Simard states, "Namaste Care is . . . a holistic end-of-life care that supports meaningful connections. . . . It affirms the individuality and enduring spirit of each person with dementia." I can also say from my reading that Namaste caregivers are trained to look for and connect with your loved one through non-verbal communication. They are encouraged and trained in the art of habilitative-oriented responses, and the program itself is structured to provide the utmost in positive sensory stimulation and physical comfort for your loved one.

I recommend getting and reading Joyce's book. While it is geared to the nursing home community–in fact written for those who wish to start a Namaste Care unit in a facility–it paints a very clear and helpful picture of how to move through the end stages of Alzheimer's with peacefulness, purpose and hope. Many practical steps and helpful tips for making those final difficult decisions are found in its chapters titled "Difficult Decisions" and "Dying and Death." Any ways in which you can enrich and fortify yourself with information and preparedness for this final stage are priceless gifts, freeing you to accept death as part of life, and allowing you to be present for your final steps together in new and richer ways. After I cried my way through these chapters, I was able to go beyond the sorrows and fears of death to celebrate and enjoy the joys that Mom and I shared each moment of our visits.

Forces....

The forces that push us
pull us
toss us
turn us
from our path,
the forces of life which last
beyond our limited view
putting us on our way to
where ever we go next . . .

Whose nature is this
that puts us betwixt
all the paths we had thought to choose?

Whose peace can this be?
Not ours, clear to see,
that calls us to struggle on
before life and vision are gone . . .
that measures each step anon
with grace, once we are done.

The journey we have been on through these pages has been filled with moments of joy and pain; filled with the agonizing wrestling of my soul—not with the inevitability of death, but with resistance to the process of dying and the means by which it comes—this last final act of being, which culminates in leaving. It has not been just our journey, Mom's and mine, that we have been on through these pages; it is everyone's—humanity's—struggle to let go. And it is the joy of discovering that letting go means receiving, having a new relationship with each other, with our loved ones, on new planes of existence, in different realities and in spirit. And in so doing we gain a deeper understanding of ourselves and them, greater unity, and the unshakable peace of being grounded with roots that go deeper than what is happening around us and to those we love. We learn to draw our strength from inner resources that are not shaken by the comings and goings of our outer world.

At the end of my part of this journey I no longer had fear of what would come next, nor experienced the level of emotional pain I used to. My place was to hold Mom gently, lightly in the here-and-now; to create joy, life and connection around her; express every beauty of life I could communicate to her through any means; and simply be with her on her journey, watching over every part of her care with as much attention as I could, using Reiki along with the support and help of hospice, her facility caregivers and the watchful eyes and hearts of all her health-care proxies. Together we wove a web of love and care around her every day.

The lessons, love and spiritual truths Mom learned on her journey were for her. They were given to her in great love from a deeper place than we normally walk in. This is part of the gift of dying—leaving. Be an agent of peace and spiritual life to your loved one, an agent of hope and joy. Sit with the dying. Clear your space until you can just be there.

And Now…

And now we wait so patiently
Like thee
Sitting in the chair of past realities
Visiting, singing, talking, bringing

Our gifts; burdened to see
A glimpse of someone who used to be.

Our stores of grief and hurt outcast
A place of emptiness and almost peace
Where all our struggles to resist have ceased.
We sit with you now
Hold your hand,
Speak in voices low and well command
Our presence to your present state of mind
A scrumptious tidbit sometimes we find.

Each visit a new journey
Into what the day will hold
Each time a brief remembrance
Of life and times of old . . .
Yet on the shrouded future-hold
Its presence yet we will not speak,
Nor nod in assent to its reach
Into our present minds.

The place we go to next—
The unknown round the bend,
Twists and turns your path will take
Where we will face the storm it makes
To sweep you out to sea,
Each wave an unknown quantity.

Will we hold fast through another toss,
Or will this next one be our loss?
And how, oh, how will we
Be calming, caring for thee

As, frightened in your course,
You face the place where you go on
And we are left behind?

Oh, how we hold on fast to keep us by your side
So you will know you're not alone,
Until you can release your ties and sail on past,
Until we all can glimpse that joy—
And you release and bid us bye;
And we let go in peace and sigh . . .
Our journey's done and safely o'er,
Where softly we stand shoulder to shoulder
Once the struggling time is over. . . .

I want to insert here another interesting note about Namaste Care. We had no knowledge of this program's existence when placing Mom, and her facility did not have the program. After reading Joyce's book, I followed her suggestions for approaching care facilities about implementing a Namaste Care program and went to see the director of nursing at Mom's care facility. She was very interested and planned to establish a Namaste Care Room for their memory care residents.

We, as caregivers, can change our corner of the world. We can introduce this program, or share our knowledge and experience with professionals working in the care industry–all to create the very best setting and care we can envision for our loved ones. We are a powerful community of family caregivers: our voices, our stories are important. I encourage you to seek information, read, and have conversations with your loved one's care providers. They are there to partner with you; you should feel comfortable speaking with people at any residence facility you choose. You should feel welcomed and listened to.

Another very important note to caregivers: Namaste Care is for you, too. Honor *your* spirit within. As you go through this debilitating, exhausting, draining time, fill your life, your heart, your soul with whatever feeds you. Surround yourself with support and caring family, friends, and professionals. Make time and space to care for yourself and let others care for you. You are the one upon whom your loved one depends. Keep yourself emotionally and physically healthy and cared for so that both of you can benefit. This part of your life will ask of you strengths and depths that, while you may rise beautifully to fill them, will drain you beyond anything you have yet experienced.

The privilege of being part of the caring, the leaving, the honoring of the spirit of your loved one is welcomed and undertaken by many caring members of the community around you. The love, knowledge, strength, and faith of this community will support you in your journey, and all this is passed through you to your loved one.

Dying is the rich, final process of a communal life and love. Open the door, open your heart—find your courage and strength:

Do not walk it alone
Yet walk your own,
Keep company on its path.
Well-worn it winds
Its own new way
To bring you home at last . . .

Namaste!

Butterfly on Blue

Epilogue

A Different Kind of Death

Float all your cares on a Silken Sea
Leave all your fears and your woes
to be free
Come Away
Come Away
Come Away on a Dream with me

One quiet Monday evening in January 2015, four days before her ninety-second birthday and surrounded by the attentive care of gentle CNAs and nurses, Mom slipped quietly into sleep and woke on angels' wings.

We were a little taken aback by this event. We had thought for sure we would know and be able to be there with her, but no, she preferred to have no fuss and bother, no bedside watch, just a gentle step off the Shores of Awake into the Sea of Infinite Possibilities. She was always a good swimmer! As soon as she was not afraid of losing touch with the ground, she could float and fly away, unfettered from her earthly stay. Once again, she has shown us the way—to let go with grace. Even in a very undignified disease, she was a lady to the last. Bless you, Mom.

Of course this makes me cry as I write it, but really, Alzheimer's is a different kind of death. After four and a half years of Mom being in nursing homes, Tom had sold their home, and Mom's things had been sorted through. My sister has her music; I have her poetry. Her remembrances have been absorbed into our homes and our lives. Her very few remaining personal items we quickly and efficiently cleared away. Now is a time of pictures and songs and memories shared. There is a terrible and beautiful relief. In the back of my mind as I go through my day, there is no longer the lingering connection to a silent woman sitting in a chair . . . or my wondering if she is getting proper care and how she manages great stretches of empty time. I now send Reiki love to accompany her on her new journey—one that I know holds more lightness and freedom and wholeness than I can imagine.

And in a strange way, I am more whole as well. This journey has imbued me with new sight, deeper wisdom and stronger courage. The Serenity Prayer says it best: the courage to accept the things I cannot change. When that happens, we find and connect with new resources to walk through dark places, and learn how to walk and live through our fears. Somewhere in the process they dissipate and leave us in a new, much wider and clearer space. What the future will hold, I do not know. Is Alzheimer's in my personal path? I do not know. Today I will celebrate the love and strength my mother's journey has imparted, and continue the bond that has grown between us past the gates of our earthly knowing.

When my time comes, as it will and however it will, she will once again be there for me as I was for her. It is the circle of our love that is unending.

Index of Poems

Beach Heart

About the Author

A lyrical poet with an individual voice and view of the world around her, Deborah Lynn is able to express and interpret her impressions, drawing upon a deep well of lifetime experience salted with the gift of being able to make a spiritual connection to joy through the pathways of emotional pain. She has the ability to clear a path, restore a vision, encourage hope and give voice to spiritual truths found in the minutiae of the everyday. Deborah is not afraid to peel back the cover of her heart. In doing so, she enables her readers to find the courage to connect to their hearts and discover their own truths.

Deborah Lynn lives in Wayland, Massachusetts with her husband and the lively memories of raising their five children scattered throughout her home in pictorial array. A late-blooming gardener, she laughingly says that she could only raise one thing at a time—children or plants. Surrounded by her beloved garden, she is situated on the border of a state park, which preserves the woods and wildlife she enjoys from her backyard. Overseen by vistas of tall pines and soaring hawks, Deborah has followed in her mother's footsteps, creating her own four-season sanctuary of living beauty inspired by her mother's enthusiastic mentoring. The very soil beneath her feet bears her mother's injection of down-home wisdom and plants, added with love, as she helped her daughter connect with the earth and realize her own garden of dreams. As a result, Deborah's roots go deep and are part of the source of her creative writing, which expresses her strong connection to earth, sky and enduring spirit. It is no wonder that the informative, compassionate look at their journey through Alzheimer's disease depicted in this book has grown from the seeds of the memories they planted together so many years ago.

Find Deborah at www.On-Angels-Wings.net find her on Facebook @OnAngelsWingsBook

About the Artists

Ellen Keiter

Design, layout; editing, nature photographs, custom ornament

Ellen Keiter is a freelance graphic design artist specializing in lettering. Studying one form of art or another in every school she attended, she finally found that graphic design–and specifically lettering–resonated most with her. She has worked with type as a phototypesetter and graphic designer, and has hand-lettered and designed everything from wedding invitations and posters to street banners, often adding detailed drawings to her designs. From her nature photos she creates high-end photographic greeting cards with inspiring messages, which she sells in local gift shops. Her love of working with words and her passion for typography have recently found expression through the art of book design. Interesting natural patterns and the beauty of this world continually inspire her. Nature has always played a large part in her life, and she often finds heart shapes wherever she goes.

Ellen lives and works in a log cabin in the woods outside Boston, surrounded by marsh, birds, chipmunks and heart-shaped rocks.

Contact Ellen at EllenatEllensArts@gmailcom.

Cheryl Rose

Cover photographs

A nature photographer since 1973, and a graduate of the School of the Museum of Fine Arts, Boston, Cheryl is captivated by every aspect of nature. She feels transported through her lens as she discovers the beauty of a dragonfly, abstract patterns in ice, or the ethereal grace of a bird in flight. In her photography, she brings us those fleeting moments when fog or light transforms a landscape into something magical, or a flock of migrating birds moves in unison creating a kaleidoscope of shapes. Her photos entice other people to observe more closely and become inspired by the beauty all around them.

Contact Cheryl Rose at Verizon.net.

Peggy McClure

Chapter Artwork

Peggy McClure is a photographer and mixed media artist living and working near Boston, Massachusetts. Drawing upon nature and life, she creates evocative images that address themes of permanence and change, loss and restoration. Her artwork from Shadows, a photography project spanning several years, is a metaphor for the passing of time, in which the subtle yet unyielding everyday changes are contrasted with the sureness of the rising sun. Forces of Nature, a mixed media series, refers to the changes over time from natural forces and from our impact on the environment. The process of layering paint and collaged images of nature, applied and scraped off multiple times, is reminiscent of the overlay of culture and nature.

Peggy McClure works at her studio in Framingham, Massachusetts and is represented by the Kingston Gallery in Boston. Visit www.peggymclure.com.

Questions for Book Discussion

Writing

- How do you think writing poetry helped Deborah throughout her caregiving challenges? How might writing help you handle your daily challenges?

Alzheimer's

- How do you feel about Alzheimer's being in your family, or how do you think you would feel if it was?
- How did Deborah's perception of the possibility of getting Alzheimer's herself change as she wrote about it?
- Do you wonder if you might get Alzheimer's? What are some ways you might look at and cope with that possibility differently after having read her story?

Caregiving

- If you are a caregiver, how is your family coping with caregiving? How has that affected your role in your family and the life of your loved one?
- If you are looking ahead to the need for caregiving in your family, what are some ways you can face the challenge?
- What are some roles and responsibilities you might want to consider?

Care Facilities

- What insights did you gain from Deborah's family's struggles with care facilities and professionals?
- How might you incorporate those insights into a search for care, should you need it for a loved one?

Memories

- How can you preserve memories of and for your loved one?
- In what positive and loving ways can you help them stay in touch with those memories?
- How would you help your family express and preserve the good and lovely relationship they have had with your loved one as he or she goes through Alzheimer's or dementia?

At Home

- In her chapter on Habilitation Therapy, Deborah discusses ways of living at home with Alzheimer's disease. How would you describe a therapeutic environment? What are some ways you can create one in your home?
- How might a therapeutic environment help you get more calmly through the day with your loved one?

Endings

- What is one new approach to living with Alzheimer's that you read about that you would like to try in your journey with your loved one, or what do you wish you had tried?
- Has reading this book helped you develop any new ideas about handling death and loss? If so, what are they for you?

Moving On

- And finally, is there life after caregiving? What might that look like?
- What will you need to help you transition back into a life centered around your *own* needs and dreams? Who or what can help you do this?

Notes

Printed in the United States
By Bookmasters